The Call of the Spirit

The Call of the Spirit

Process Spirituality in a Relational World

Reissued with a New Preface from
Marjorie Hewitt Suchocki

John B. Cobb, Jr.
Bruce G. Epperly
Paul S. Nancarrow

Introduction and Afterword
Marjorie Hewitt Suchocki

ANOKA, MINNESOTA 2022

The Call of the Spirit: Process Spirituality in a Relational World
Faith in Process Series

© 2022 Process Century Press

All rights reserved. Except for brief quotations in critical publications and reviews, no part of this book may be reproduced in any manner without prior permission from the publisher.

Scripture quotations are from Revised Standard Version of the Bible, copyright © 1946, 1952, and 1971 National Council of the Churches of Christ in the United States of America. Used by permission. All rights reserved worldwide.

Process Century Press
RiverHouse LLC
802 River Lane
Anoka, MN 55303

Process Century Press books are published in association with the International Process Network.

Cover: Susanna Mennicke

Originally published in 2005 by P&F Press, Claremont, CA.

VOLUME: II
FAITH IN PROCESS SERIES
JEANYNE B. SLETTOM, GENERAL EDITOR

ISBN 978-1-940447-56-8
Printed in the United States of America

SERIES PREFACE: FAITH IN PROCESS

Alfred North Whitehead's process philosophy develops and explores the concept that all existence is necessarily relational. Nothing is isolated: all things are interconnected. Such theories are now commonplace in many of the sciences, but they are also deeply resonant with religious and theological thought. Perhaps the most profound religious expression of process thinking is the necessarily interrelational nature of all things, not only to one another, but also and centrally to God. Internally and externally, we exist in and through relationships. Many forms of process theologies have been developed in the decades since relational thinking deepened our understanding of reality.

Process Century Press has published a number of works dealing with relational thought. But theoretical work has not been the only mode of working with the relational structure of all existence—to the contrary, many practical implications have also affected personal and communal forms of religion. In this Faith in Process series, the Press looks to contemporary resources that enhance religious life, both personally and communally. It may well be that there is no greater need for such works than our present time. Given the flux in the contemporary world—the merging of politics and faith, renewed questions about who "qualfiies" to lead religious activities, tensions between freedom and responsibility, the scope of freedom for women and their own bodies, issues of migration, continuing racism—there are issues enough! Relational forms of thinking are needed now more than ever. And because we are indeed relational, interwoven with one another at our deepest levels, it may even be possible that works exploring and promoting our relationships to one another and to God may be part and parcel of our healing.

Marjorie Hewitt Suchocki

OTHER BOOKS IN THIS SERIES

Praying with Process Theology, Bruce G. Epperly
The Call of the Spirit, John B. Cobb, Jr., Bruce Epperly, Paul S. Nancarrow
Mystery without Magic, Russell Pregeant
Jesus Learns to Glow (picture book), Timothy Murphy and C.J. Ward

Contents

Preface to the 2022 Edition

Introduction, 1
Marjorie Hewitt Suchocki

Part One

1. Whitehead's Model and Multiple Spiritualities, 11
   John B. Cobb, Jr.

2. Pathways to Spiritual Transformation, 27
   Bruce G. Epperly

3. Communal Spiritual Practice in Ceremony and Liturgy, 41
   Paul S. Nancarrow

Part Two

4. Spirituality and Sensory Perception, 59
   John B. Cobb, Jr.

5. An Adventurous Spirituality, 73
   Bruce G. Epperly

6. A Spirituality of Discernment, 87
   Paul S. Nancarrow

Part Three

7. Whitehead and Spiritual Discipline, 105
   John B. Cobb, Jr.

8. A Spirituality of Compassion, 121
   Bruce G. Epperly

9. Compassion in Communion, 133
   Paul S. Nancarrow

Afterword, 147
   Marjorie Hewitt Suchocki

# Preface to the 2022 Edition

Marjorie Hewitt Suchocki

Some years ago, I wrote an introduction to this fine collection of essays, delineating the differences of perspective the three primary authors presented, and the deep interrelationships between the disparate essays. There was a fine blending in the way the three authors complemented one another's work, producing a rich and varied interpretation of the call of the Spirit.

But assumptions about the world most people shared in the early part of this twenty-first century have radically changed. In those earlier years we lived in a world where truth could easily be discerned from falsehood, where newspapers and broadcasts shared common assumptions about fact and fiction. Yes, one could predictably discern liberal and conservative biases, but these were obvious and expected. They interpreted but did not undermine given facts. For the most part, we lived in a world of shared public experience underlying our personal differences. Ah, what a faraway world that now seems!

Another assumption—perhaps uneasily held—concerned

our changing climate. John B. Cobb Jr. sounded the alarm in his small book, *Is It Too Late?* The book, written in 1969 and published in 1971, called radical attention to climate change. Thirty years later Al Gore dramatized the problem in his film, "An Inconvenient Truth." But the vast response was more like complacency than alarm. Yes, there were climate changes, but for the most part we considered them subtle rather than alarming. Indeed, in Southern California we celebrated the result of tightened regulations regarding gasoline for our cars—we could see the mountains again; we could breathe more easily! Yes, there was global warming—but weren't we doing something about it? Alas, how faraway now that easy optimism seems.

In this decade of the 2020s we live in a new reality, riven by "fake news" and "conspiracy theories" and outright threats to democracy in this the oldest of democracies. "Truth" is no longer a commonly agreed upon state of affairs; to the contrary, "truth" seems to be whatever commodity best serves one's political or financial purposes. But how do we effectively communicate with one another when there is no agreed upon "reality," let alone "truth"? Must we agree only on superficial things when the deep things of the spirit have no resting place in a world of variegated "truth"?

And what of spirituality in a world gone amok through unmitigated climate change? Has our complacency of the past led us only to paralysis in the present? What is spirituality in a time when we can no longer get away with singing "God is the ruler yet," as though we could expect God to clean up all the plastic we have put into the ocean? How can we sing "for the beauty of the Earth" when through our actions beauty dies like the vanishing monarch butterflies; when summers literally burn our landscapes with raging flames, and our cities and countryside burn with triple-digit heat? What happens to environmental expectations when storms occur where no such storms have ever occurred before, and where tornadoes have over two hundred miles of touching ground to strew wreckage across several states?

Is the call of the Spirit the same in times such as these? I ask you now to read these essays again, in today's world. Read them against the tragedies of the "loss of truth" and the now clearly devastating world of climate change. Read them to see again the truths of God calling us to responsible stewardship in the world we now know; read them to see that "rationality" and "spirituality" are complements rather than opposites; read them to refresh your spirit. Read them to once again hear, clearly, the "call of the Spirit." Be refreshed, and answer the call.

Acknowledgement

The authors acknowledge with gratitude the superb contributions of P&F Press editor, Jeanyne B. Slettom. She inspired us with her original vision for the book, and with competence and zeal she organized, coordinated, and edited our writings. We are fortunate to be blessed with so gifted an editor.

INTRODUCTION

Marjorie Hewitt Suchocki

"SPIRITUALITY" in contemporary culture often functions as a code word substituting for the more institutional sounding word, "religious." Used in this way, "spirituality" suggests that institutional religion refers to external practices rather than to the inward subjective experience of union with a mystery beyond ourselves. But the profound exploration of spirituality in this book gives the lie to any hard and fast separation of the external and the internal, the objective and the subjective, the institutional and the private, the political and the personal. In place of such false separations, the three writers of *The Call of the Spirit* show how the integration of these elements is necessary if we are to reach any degree of fulfillment of the human yearning for connection to God and neighbor.

By framing spirituality as connection to God and neighbor, we must beware of reducing this openness solely to individualistic terms. We dare not reduce "neighbor" to one's personal neighbor, the "person next door." The parable of the Good Samaritan insists that the neighbor is precisely the one—indeed, the many—in need, even when we do not know these persons by name. Openness to the neighbor's good entails a responsible care for social, cultural, and political systems, holding them to the critique of the good of the "neighbor." A spirituality of openness to the other necessarily involves political awareness of what makes for the good of the other, and actions conforming to this awareness.

Spirituality is ultimately about connection, relation. It entails a deepening and widening of one's inner experience that is only possible through opening oneself to that which is other. Ordinarily, we think of this spiritual opening of the self in terms of an opening to God, and spirituality is certainly about that. But in a thoroughly relational world one cannot be open solely to God. Indeed, to increase one's openness to God involves, at the same time, a deeper attentiveness to the world around us. Openness to God entails openness to the neighbor—human or otherwise—and openness to the neighbor entails openness to God. As John Wesley so famously said, "One of the principal rules of religion is to lose no occasion of serving God. And, since God is invisible to our eyes, we are to serve God in our neighbor, which God receives as if done to God in person, standing visibly before us."[1] Spirituality is the integration of the experience of the Other and the others into the depths of the self, and a consequent giving of the self to the Other and others in responsible (and "response-able") living. In and through this giving and receiving, the self is continuously formed as spirit.

In a sense, of course, every instance of the self is a receiving of otherness into the becoming of the self, an integration of this reception, and a consequent giving of the self in influence to others, over and over again. We live in this process of receiving, integrating, and giving in every moment of our lives. But as we know too well, it is possible to live very shallow lives. Too easily we can subordinate the legitimate integrity of the other to our own ends, taking only that which we judge to promote our own advantage, and exercising our influence so as to increase what we perceive to be our own benefit regardless of the welfare of others. We can live as if all relationships begin and end with our own personal good. Spirituality seeks to overcome this.

Spirituality, then, involves a yearning to overcome smallness of being, to develop a wideness of personality that lives and acts toward a good greater than one's own. How we even perceive "the good" expands to include the welfare of the whole insofar as we can imagine it, always with the sense that our imaginings fall short. Spirituality of this sort necessarily increases one's openness to others, incorporating their own well-being into one's own and even critiquing one's understanding of "goodness" through what is learned through the other.

In a relational world, spirituality inescapably involves us in a deeper openness to God, whether we know it or not. God is that One who relates intentionally to all creatures, including ourselves. The relationship is always toward our good, but is usually experienced subliminally, deeper than our consciousness normally allows. God is the ever-present Companion. But there is a certain incognito quality in God's relating to us, precisely because God's influence is always toward our best way of being in the world. Ironically, perhaps, we do not notice God because God points us toward the world, not toward Godself. If we are attentive to the call of God, then we are remarkably involved in the world around us. This is why we can say that by opening ourselves to the good of others, we are opening ourselves to the influence of God.

Yet we long for more than this. We want the Giver, and not

just the gift—we want a conscious sense of our connection to this God who calls us. Our spirits call out for God's Spirit, so that we might breathe this sense of connection into our deepest selves. We don't want "God Incognito," we want to experience the reality of God insofar as we finite creatures are able. We want to taste the immensity of God as love, experiencing God's love for ourselves as well as for all others. The peculiarity of such feelings is in the paradox, perhaps best expressed in Christopher Marlowe's wonderful phrase from *The Jew of Malta*, "so infinite a treasure in so small a space." It seems we cannot bear too much of God.

Spirituality, then, in a relational world, lives in, with, and toward the mystery of God and others. There is something of God in us, an influence toward the good that includes the good of others. There is something of all other creatures in us as well, breathings from the past that we take into ourselves in every moment. Who we are rests with our integration of these "othernesses," and with the growth of our capacity to be more and more open to these "othernesses." As we integrate them into the becoming of each of our moments, we increase as well the magnitude of our givingness. In this receiving, integrating, and giving is our spirituality, born again and again in each moment.

These are but brief reflections on the nature of spirituality, on what happens in our responses to the call of the Spirit. This book is a profound expansion of such reflections, developed—as is appropriate in a relational world—through the cooperative writings of three remarkable persons. John B. Cobb, Jr., the world's foremost process theologian, develops the relational dynamics of spirituality. His essays are followed by those of Bruce Epperly and Paul Nancarrow, each of whom focuses on the experiential side of spirituality. Epperly, seminary professor and contributor of regular essays on spirituality for Process & Faith's quarterly journal, *Creative Transformation*, develops the experiential side of spirituality as it relates to personal disciplines. Paul Nancarrow, pastor, teacher, and also a contributor to *Creative Transformation*, shows the communal nature of spirituality, particularly as expressed in the liturgy of the Church.

The book is structured in three parts. In Part One, our three authors speak generally about the personal and social structure of spirituality. John B. Cobb, Jr. lays out the process of relationships that undergirds the writings of all three authors, and indeed, of most process theologians. He shows how the dynamics of a relational world can yield a variety of forms of spirituality, each of which evolves within the cultural milieu of its origins. Yet these differences do not negate the fundamental reality that spirituality necessarily entails an increasing openness to that which is other.

In this same first section, Bruce Epperly focuses on the relational dynamics that allow us the possibility of becoming open to the experience of the God who is constantly present. Epperly suggests practices to enhance this experience, such as a focus on mind/body unity, breath prayers, and walking prayers. In a relational world, mind and body are an integrated unity; hence spirituality can be deepened by attention to our physical nature as it impacts our psychic nature. Indeed, that which we usually distinguish as our "psychic" self depends upon its relation to the "physical" self, and God relates as much to us through the one as through the other. Thus attenuation to God can be strengthened in and through disciplined bodily practices.

Paul Nancarrow concludes this section by complementing Epperly's personal approach with the communal experience of people gathered together for worship. Given that spirituality involves openness to the other, this communal emphasis necessarily follows. Ritual, ceremony, and liturgy are spiritual paths taking place in the community, paralleling more individual disciplines. But, like Epperly's development of the role of the body in personal disciplines, Nancarrow focuses on the physicality of communal disciplines. Whether it is the adoption of bodily postures, or smelling incense, or tasting wine and bread, or feeling water, the whole body is involved in its participation with the larger body of Christ. The community is an organic whole, involving the whole personhood of its participants, body and soul.

Part Two focuses on the dynamics of perception. That is, spirituality is openness to God and others. This openness is a drawing into the self of that which is felt through the other; it is a mode of perception that enlarges our spirit. Cobb expands upon his introductory essay in Part One by going into greater detail concerning a relational understanding of how perception takes place. To do this, he utilizes not only the relational dynamics of Alfred North Whitehead's process philosophy, but also the theological writings of John Wesley. Wesley, like Whitehead, understood God to be pervasively present to each reality in the universe; Wesley, like Whitehead, understood the effects of God's presence to be persuasive rather than determinative; Wesley, like Whitehead, understood that God's influence actually creates the freedom through which the creature responsibly determines its response to the influence of God. By utilizing Wesley as well as Whitehead, Cobb writes from the fullness of his own spirituality, for Cobb's life integrates the influences of both great thinkers.

Epperly picks up the conversation by focusing on practices that heighten our perception of the universally present God. To sense God is to sense a call to a new future in every moment; there is adventure involved in developing our spirituality, our openness to the call of the Spirit. Utilizing prayers of encircling, holy imagination, holy reading, and affirmative awareness,

Epperly gives concrete suggestions for how we might move with the dynamics of perception developed by Cobb, heightening our growth in the spirit.

In Nancarrow's contribution, he, too, speaks of communal ways of heightening our perception of God's presence and call. Cobb had raised the question of distinguishing God's call from the many competing voices in every moment of experience. Nancarrow introduces the ancient concept of discernment, developed within community, as enhancing our perception of God. In his previous chapter, Nancarrow focused on the liturgical practices of communal worship; here he focuses on small group experiences of working together to discern the call of the Spirit. Because God always calls the individual in the particularities of context, God's call always has a communal as well as individual aspect. Those within our community, then, can offer insight in the discernment process.

Nancarrow extends these insights by using the concept of discernment within the context of community for a variety of settings. Initially, a small group gathered for spiritual growth, and/or mutual support can assist each individual within the group. But Nancarrow also speaks of group discernment—called "the check-in"—as a device used just prior to worship in order to ready the congregation for the communal act of worship. Finally, he outlines a structure that can be used in group Bible study to enhance our sense of God's leading. He concludes his chapter with suggestions for how to develop spiritual direction for groups. Ordinarily spiritual direction is understood as a one-on-one discipline, but Nancarrow effectively shows how spiritual direction can capitalize on the communal nature of God's call, leading the group as well as each person into deeper modes of spirituality.

Appropriately, this book concludes with a focus on compassion developed in Part Three. Spirituality in a relational world opens us to God and to others. We take the situations of others into ourselves, feeling their joy or sorrow, fulfillment or need, health or illness. Since God is with all persons, to feel the other is also to be open to a feeling of God with the other, but as Cobb points out, the first does not require sensitivity to the second. That is, while it is so that God is with the other, secular modes of spiritual openness to the other do not necessarily extend to the experience of God's role in the other. Remember, in a process world God usually operates "incognito," hidden within the directive force toward the world's good. God can call persons toward forms of spirituality that focus exclusively on care for the world.

Yet by and large, what we usually mean by "spirituality" includes sensitivity to the presence of God. Once again, Cobb masterfully takes us into the dynamics of process thought whereby we can discern God at work. And this work is to increase our compassion for creatures, human and otherwise, and to act accordingly. Spirituality is an active rather than passive quality. Given God's compassionate care for all creatures, our own increase of compassion—whether secular or religious—aligns us with God's concerns. And since God works *with* the world rather than *on* the world, our growth in compassionate living contributes to the achievement of God's own purposes in the world.

Epperly's development of a "spirituality of compassion" again leads us into very practical disciplines for nurturing a compassionate spirit. These include centering prayer, seeing into new possibilities even in the midst of trouble ("finding angels in boulders"), seeing Christ in every person we meet—particularly those in need—and cultivating an attitude of "mending the world." This last discipline includes imaginative ways of "praying the world," which is to align ourselves with God's own care for this world's good.

Nancarrow concludes the section, and, indeed, the book as a

whole, with his essay on "communion in compassion." The focus of the Christian practice of Eucharist, or Holy Communion, or the Lord's Supper—whatever it be called—is our conformation to the One we call Lord. We are brought into living connection with the Jesus proclaimed to us in the gospels so that we may have his mind in us. This liturgy, experienced together as Christ's body, takes us also into the Jesus of the gospels. His table fellowship embraces us, so that by extension we are included in that company of tax collectors, prostitutes, publicans, scribes, and Pharisees who sat at one time or another at table with him. This inclusion, now at the Communion table, unites us with his intensity of care for the well-being of all. Being one with him, we are mingled together into that quality of compassion. Receiving his compassion, we are impelled to live compassionately.

Nancarrow richly develops the many nuances that are both implicit and explicit in the symbolic elements of this uniquely Christian experience of table fellowship with the Lord. Ultimately, this table fellowship recalls and re-enacts Jesus' self-offering to God in and through his self-offering to others. As such, it draws us into this self-offering, now extended to the world in and through us. Communion is for the sake of compassion.

It is highly appropriate that *The Call of the Spirit* concludes with these three essays giving three different perspectives—metaphysical, personal, communal—on a spirituality of compassion. We are thoroughly constituted by our creative response to the relationships that inform us, and these relationships include God and the vast multiplicity of influences from the world. We are assured in the Christian scriptures that "God so loved the world," that God's care for the world is an intensity of care for the world's well-being, which is to say, righteousness, justice. We see this care carried out in the ministry of Jesus, perhaps typified in the recurrent phrase, "he had compassion on the multitude." In a process relational world, to love God is to be swept up into God's own love for the world, God's care for its well-being. It is to become a participant in God's great compassion. To develop spirituality in this relational world of ours is to develop a habit of attentiveness to the call of the Spirit, which will lead us ever more deeply into lives that are marked by the compassion of God.

These nine essays form an integral whole, combining a careful analysis of relational dynamics with very practical suggestions for personal and communal ways of intensifying our spirituality. The essays flow from the wellsprings of spirituality in each of our authors; they are "lived" essays, and not simply theoretical discussions. To read the essays, then, is to be invited into the privilege of seeing how the call of the Spirit has been answered in each of these three lives. One can join with them by reading this book meditatively, reflecting on one's own responses to the issues named. But one can also read this book as a kind of manual, giving tested instruction for persons and for communities to focus intentionally on increasing our spiritual awareness. In this sense, then, perhaps the book functions according to its apt title—it may, indeed, represent for us the call of the Spirit.

Notes

1. John Wesley, *A Plain Account of Christian Perfection* (Kansas City: Beacon Hill, 1966), 111.

PART ONE

1

Whitehead's Model and Multiple Spiritualities

John B. Cobb, Jr.

2

Pathways to Spiritual Transformation

Bruce G. Epperly

3

Communal Spiritual Practice in Ceremony and Liturgy

Paul S. Nancarrow

ONE

Whitehead's Model and Multiple Spiritualities

John B. Cobb, Jr.

"SPIRITUALITY" is a term that returned to our central vocabulary about twenty-five years ago. My first reaction was critical. I feared its individualistic emphasis and its close connection with a consumerist culture. It seemed quite alien to the Bible. It had its roots in the monastery, and Luther had rejected it in favor of "faith." It sounded very much like the "religion" of which Karl Barth was so critical. Why should Protestants now seize it with such enthusiasm? Was it not better to emphasize discipleship?

On the other hand, as a process theologian I could not fail to be interested in experience. That is what process thought is all about. And the renewed interest in spirituality was, in part, an insistence that actual experience is important. The concern underlying it was the unsatisfactory character of ordinary experience for so many people and the need for a transformation of that experience. A process theologian could well share that concern.

Accordingly, I tried to work with the new interest in spirituality. I taught courses and wrote articles on the subject, hoping to broaden the concept so that we could recognize that our self-giving involvement with other people in the world could be understood as profoundly spiritual. I argued that the human spirit should be understood both in its distinctiveness and in its intimate connection to other dimensions of the human psyche. I called for an integrated personal existence centering in the spirit, understanding the human spirit in a Niebuhrian way as the capacity for self-objectification or self-transcendence. I argued that true Christian spirituality involved global consciousness.

But my efforts to enlarge or extend or transform what students meant by "spirituality" had little success. What people wanted and identified in this way was something very individual and interior. The hunger for spirituality was a reaction to the immersion in a world of others, with all the pressures and irritations such immersion places in our way. Public life and social responsibility needed some counterpoint in privacy and inner discipline. This was what was called, and called for as, "spirituality."

Since this was what Protestants in general had turned away from centuries earlier, it is not surprising that the older Protestant churches (with the partial exception of the Quakers) were not in a good position to respond. This was not because most American Protestant churches had kept alive the Reformation understanding of faith. Instead, they had come to understand the interior life in psychological terms and, to a considerable extent, had substituted these terms for the vocabulary of faith. But the quest for spirituality could not be identified with the quest for psychological health. Furthermore, Protestant church life was based on community, and most Protestant worship had minimal space for individual interiority. With the decline of pietism, the American churches had largely given up on instructing their members in private religious disciplines. As a result, more and more people said they were spiritual but not religious, meaning that what they found in ordinary Protestant church life seemed largely irrelevant to their spiritual hunger.

If the meaning of spirituality is inescapably wed to the emphasis on the individual, the private, and the interior, then one may deplore its limitations, but one need not minimize its importance. Regardless of the history of Protestantism, there is no question but that privacy and individuality and inner discipline can play an important part in human life. What we do with our interiority can be damaging as well as helpful; so we should not celebrate all forms of spirituality. But clearly spirituality calls for our attention.

In developing my own understanding of Christianity in general and Christian spirituality in particular, I have found the philosophy of Alfred North Whitehead particularly useful. I believe that it supports the values of many contemporary Christians. For me it clarifies the elements in experience that contemporary Christians most prize and also makes clearer how they can be accentuated and developed. Accordingly, I will sketch Whitehead's basic model of human experience before proceeding further.

Process theology is the model of reality that underlies my discussion of several spiritualities. The world is made up of events, not "things" as they are usually understood. A momentary human experience is the kind of event to which we have immediate access. Such a moment draws together features of the world it inherits, especially its own past and events in the body. Through these, and also more immediately, human experience is influenced by other people and the natural world. The experience occurs and passes, becoming part of the world that flows into future experiences.

Personal experience consists of a flow of such momentary

experiences. The successors inherit with special fullness from past moments of this flow. A person is quite distinct from other persons and things. Yet it is equally important to recognize that the relation to one's own past is not fundamentally different from the relation to others. Persons are members one of another. We participate in constituting one another. We are all social products.

It is equally important to see that although we are largely constituted by the past that flows into each momentary experience, we are not simply the product of that past. In each moment there is something more. There is a decision about how to order and supplement the received past. That is where freedom and novelty appear. That decision is possible only because each occasion not only inherits from the past but also receives novel possibilities for its own constitution. This is God's presence in the occasion. God calls us to be and do what is best in the very concrete and limited situations in which we find ourselves. Our task is to respond fully to God's call.

With this Whiteheadian model presupposed, what do we find when we attend to spirituality? The first thing that becomes evident is its great diversity. There are many proposals as to how best to form our interior lives. Some people have explored one after another. Others tout one, and one alone, as right for all. In general, judgments are determined by how the various practices make the practitioner feel. But some are convinced of the rightness of one practice even though they understand that the payoff might be long postponed. The single coherent lens of process thought may make it easier to judge among these options or to see how they can be combined.

Let us begin with Buddhism. Whereas the Bible and the Abrahamic traditions are not primarily to be understood as forms of spirituality and do not make spirituality central to the ways of life they propose, Buddhism can reasonably be understood as focused on spirituality. Each school of Buddhism has its distinctive meditational practices and disciplines; so a Buddhist scholar could devote many lectures to this diversity. I am not a scholar of Buddhism, and I will limit myself to some sweeping generalizations that probably do not apply to all forms of Buddhism. It is enough for me if they do apply to some major forms that Westerners have found attractive.

The Buddhist goal is to experience reality as it really is. Buddhists are convinced that this enlightenment is profoundly liberating. We live in a world of illusion, and much of what is lacking and painful in our lives results from this distortion. To be free from this is to attain wisdom and compassion.

Buddhism is particularly attractive to a Whiteheadian because its teaching about reality is so congenial. Buddhist schools agree in rejecting the idea of substance that is so pervasively built into our language and perceptual habits. We see ourselves as surrounded by long-lasting objects such as tables and human bodies and trees and other people. We project meanings on these and attach ourselves to them. Since, in fact, nothing is permanent, this leads to suffering.

Still more seriously, we experience ourselves as substances enduring through time. As a result, we feel guilt and shame for past actions and anxiety about what we will do and what will happen to us in the future. We try to hold on to what we have, and we feel threatened by others. We project all kinds of meanings on ourselves as well as on other people, meanings that lead to disappointment or humiliation.

In reality, all is in flux. Nothing exists in and of itself. Each momentary event is the coming together of the world at that point. This process is named *pratitya samutpada,* which can be translated as "dependent origination." When we truly realize what we are—and what the world is—that is, when we actually experience the world, and ourselves, in this way, we are freed of all attachment and attain a blessed serenity and freedom.

There are many disciplines that help move us in this direction. One is that of simple attention to what is taking place in experience at each moment. One notes what is happening and, instead of letting it shape one's feelings, one lets it go. The experience is the togetherness of these feelings, and if one releases them, then the next moment of experience can be what it is without the burden of interpretation.

To demonstrate the difference between this kind of experience and ordinary experience, I like to tell the story of an experiment conducted in a Catholic university in Tokyo several decades ago. Representatives of three groups were selected and hooked up to devices to measure brain activity. One group was of people like me, who engage in prayer and meditation without special disciplines. The second group was composed of practitioners of Vedantic yoga. The third was a group of Zen nuns.

All were asked to engage in their normal practice. Then after a few minutes a raucous buzzer was sounded for a few seconds. A few minutes later, and then at irregular intervals, this was repeated. The question was how the members of the three groups would react.

The first group reacted as a psychologist would expect—quite strongly the first time and with diminishing intensity subsequently. The yogis did not react at all. The Buddhists reacted a little to the first buzz and just the same to the subsequent ones.

The explanation is evident. Undisciplined people like me who are trying to concentrate on their prayers are quite irritated by an unpleasant sound. We are annoyed by its repetitions as well, but we gradually accustom ourselves to them and take them in stride, knowing that they are part of the experiment. The yogis, in marked contrast, have shut out the exterior world and its stimuli altogether. They cultivate a consciousness that separates them from the surrounding world. The Buddhists are attentive to all that happens but simply let it happen as it happens. They are free from any other goal than to let things be what they are. They attach no meaning to the raucous noise beyond its sheer occurrence. Hence they respond to it in just the same way each time.

Buddhists can accent other implications of their basic ontology. Thus far I have emphasized the "no self" doctrine and impermanence. Buddhists can also speak of the True Self. The True Self is the all-inclusive self. That is, at each moment one includes the world. There is no separation between the private self and the remainder of things. Thus one's true interests are the interests of all. Selfishness and self-centeredness disappear with the illusion of the false self and are replaced by universal compassion.

There are still other directions in which one may move that have been less emphasized in Buddhist circles. One is a kind of nature mysticism. If my experience in each moment consists of the many others, and most of these are not human, I can experience myself as part of the natural world. This kind of realization has probably been more important in the West, because most of our religious and philosophical traditions have alienated us from nature. The less alienated East does not require special disciplines to help people locate themselves within nature.

I should make it clear that Buddhists know there is a strong tendency to identify ourselves as persons existing through time. They have shown, rightly from a Whiteheadian perspective, that, in fact, there is no strict identity of personal existence. There is a new experience in each moment, and there is no substance underlying these experiences. But Buddhists do not question that ordinarily there is a very close relationship between successive moments of personal existence. Popular doctrines of karma, in particular, presuppose this continuity through time. Buddhist disciplines, however, work to weaken this connection because, Buddhists think, this strong connection is based on illusory beliefs and is a root cause of suffering.

From a Whiteheadian perspective, the absence of any substantial identity through time does not necessarily lead to disparaging an emphasis on personal identity. We do inherit most of what we are in each moment from antecedent moments of personal experience. Although much of this inheritance is damaging, much of it can also be beneficial. There can, therefore, be spiritualities based on enduring personal existence in distinction from those that focus on momentary existence.

Some of these emphasize interpersonal relations. There is a Native American saying that we should not judge another until we have walked for two days in the other's moccasins. The discipline required here is, of course, imaginative identification with the other. What is it like to be where the other is, with that person's responsibilities and hopes, that person's biography, that person's network of relationships?

Such discipline is relevant not only to judging others. It is also an intense expression of love. In less costly ways, one can discipline oneself to think of each other person one encounters as a subject, a center of experience, rather than in terms of how that person appears to oneself. One can extend this to other living things. By emphasizing otherness as well as relationship, this differs from the typical Buddhist sense of the true self in its inclusion of all. The point here is that the other is not an object to the self but a subject like oneself deserving of the same care and concern. This way of thinking requires the affirmation of the positive value of continuity in the formation of personal existence.

The discipline I have described aims in part to make oneself as a person more understanding of others and more loving. This presupposes the possibility of cumulative spiritual growth. Of course, there are other ways in which one may want to grow. One may aim to broaden one's horizons and deepen one's analysis, so that one may be more effective in acting for the common good. One may aim to overcome fears and anxieties that block one's expression of love. One may aim to become better able to receive from others even when that makes one more vulnerable. There are many, many goals of spiritual growth with their accompanying disciplines.

One important discipline of spiritual growth has been developed under the influence of Carl Jung. This is based on an elaborate analysis of the depths of the psyche. It is sometimes explained in terms that reify archetypes and other elements of the psyche in ways that a process theologian cannot accept. However, the phenomena lend themselves to a Whiteheadian explanation and, quite independently of Whitehead, some Jungians have moved in this direction.

In Whitehead's view the entire past plays some role in the formation of each occasion of human experience. The most important part of this past is the human past. Within that past, some patterns have been repeated in human experience millions of times. These repetitions cumulatively constitute this pattern as distinctively effective in each of the occasions of experience that inherits from them. In depth analysis, one can find images, or archetypes, expressive of these patterns. Through spiritual maturation these archetypes come to play different roles in the individual's psychic life.

The spiritualities I have described thus far are primarily mind disciplines. There are others that emphasize the body. This makes good sense for a Whiteheadian, since the integrated flow of experience that we think of as ourselves derives most of its content from events in the body. To change the body is to change experience. To achieve a relaxed and harmonious bodily condition enables the body to contribute to the well-being of the psyche and even to the attainment of extraordinary psychic states. One can derive from Whitehead's model no detailed knowledge of what bodily postures and movements are most conducive to desired states of the psyche, only that this is a topic well worth exploring. This exploration has been carried furthest in India and China.

Whereas in India and China the relation of mind and body is generally understood as interactive and holistic, the emphasis on bodily determination of the psyche in the West can lead to chemical manipulation of experience. Instead of engaging in time-consuming disciplines, Westerners are prone to seek to change experience by taking drugs. In most cases these are ingested, but it is also possible to find practices that cause the body to produce them naturally.

There is no doubt that drugs alter experience. There is also no reason, from a Whiteheadian perspective, to suppose that what is experienced in this way is unreal. On the contrary, Whitehead showed that our ordinary experience obscures the deeper relationships that form us in order to highlight that to which we need to attend for practical purposes. Some chemically altered states of consciousness appear to bring to the fore the deeper experience that has been overlaid and obscured by evolutionary processes.

The intimate relation of psyche to body depicted in Whitehead's model allows us to understand and encourage spiritualities that focus on the other direction of this relationship. Especially in the nineteenth and twentieth century, reflecting the influence of idealistic philosophy, the condition of the psyche has been shown to affect the condition of the body. Thoroughgoing idealists argue that the body itself has no existence independent of the mind, so that changing one's thought can solve any problem in the body. Whiteheadians have little patience for this extreme view. For us, bodily events are just as real as psychic ones. But just as bodily events profoundly influence psychic ones, so also psychic events profoundly influence bodily ones. Psychic or spiritual healing is a reality, and we are open to believing even quite astounding claims about the effects of psychic activity on physical processes in the body.

Thus far I have described spiritualities that are nontheistic or, at least, not dependent on a theistic understanding. It is important for theists to recognize the variety and richness of such spiritualities. We have in the past sometimes so identified spirituality with the relation of the individual to God that we have failed to recognize the many valuable forms of spirituality that do not depend on belief in God, even though some of them sometimes lead to that belief.

Nevertheless, Whitehead's model gives a large place to God and to human experience of God. It is time to turn to that dimension of the model and to the spiritualities it explains and supports.

So far I have noted how the many become one in each momentary experience. In personal existence, the most determinative are usually those from one's personal past and the events in the person's body. This allows, as noted, for spiritualities that take more seriously the otherness of other persons, more so than Buddhism usually does. It encourages the I-thou spiritualities more characteristic of the West as well as the psychosomatic ones richly developed in China and India.

But Whitehead emphasizes that the many that become one in each moment are not limited to the past occasions that make up the world for each new experience. If they were, then the present experience could be nothing more than the product of the past. There would be nothing left for the new occasion to decide. There could be no freedom and no real novelty. Something else enters into the composition of each new occasion of experience. Whitehead calls this God.

God's role in each occasion is to offer it possibilities not derived from the past but relevant to that past. God calls each human occasion of experience to actualize the richest possibility in that new moment. This richness is both for immediate enjoyment and for its contribution to the future.

If God is calling us moment by moment, this suggests a spirituality of discernment. How can we distinguish that within our experience which is God's call from the many competing voices that are derived from the past?

We should not overstate the problem. On the whole, one who seeks to respond to others in love and to serve the common good generally knows what to do. The Whiteheadian point is that this knowledge is not entirely rational. One does not simply follow rules. One often senses more than one can explain. The disciplines of love discussed above increase that sensitivity and the ability to respond beyond one's conscious knowledge. Believers in God as known in Jesus Christ are not left in blank ignorance of what they are called to do and be, and a Whiteheadian can suppose that as one orients oneself toward others there is subtle but effective, largely unconscious, guidance from God. Since God's guidance is primarily moment by moment, it calls for spontaneity more than for spiritual disciplines.

Nevertheless, Christians have every reason to desire clearer guidance and greater assurance that the intuitions they follow are of God. Those who follow disciplines designed to open themselves to such guidance have contributed much. Two groups have developed methods that seem particularly appropriate to a Whiteheadian: the Jesuits and the Quakers. In both cases an attitude of open receptivity is cultivated. The assumption, as with Whiteheadians, is that God is immediately present and directive. It is also assumed that the discrimination of God's call from all the hunches, prejudices, hopes, and ambitions that flood experience is not easy, but, still, is possible.

Both also make another assumption that seems very appropriate to a Whiteheadian. Although discrimination is possible, it is never certain. Our capacities for self-deception are great. The deeply inward individual quest for guidance is followed by sharing in the community. The individual should take the response of the community very seriously. Individual idiosyncrasies are less likely to shape the community judgment. Of course, there is nothing infallible about this either. This spirituality of discernment reflects the normal condition of Christian believers. Although God is present in every occasion of experience, God is not the one who decides. The occasion decides how fully it is to be informed by God's call. Hence, there is a clear distinction between the human self and God. The focus is on God's purpose for one's life.

There are other forms of theistic spirituality that seek to experience God in God's more inclusive actuality. These are often called mystical. Fully mystical experience is much less common than the sense of being called and guided. But for a Whiteheadian its occurrence is understandable. God is, in fact, being felt in every occasion. For the most part that feeling unconsciously objectifies God in terms of the divine aim for the occasion. But there is no necessity that God be felt only in that way. Some report occasions on which a presence is felt, reassuring and loving. Sometimes this comes abruptly as a pure gift, but there are also those who practice disciplines designed to make such experience more likely.

Mystical experience can seek another result, one of identity. This is more problematic both from a biblical point of view and a Whiteheadian one. But a Whiteheadian can understand a condition that could be interpreted in this way.

In the spirituality of discernment, it was clear that the center of the human experience is distinct from the role that God plays in that experience. The goal is to distinguish God's call from all else with the intention that decisions be guided by God. But it is not impossible that God's presence in the occasion play the role of decision-maker. There would then be no "I" distinct from God. The occasion's deciding center would be God. The feeling of union with God in this sense would not be an illusion.

These distinctively theistic forms of spirituality are not necessarily more appropriate for Christians than the nontheistic ones. We are called to serve our neighbors. In doing so we serve God. Finding ways to attain the inner peace we need in order to be effective in this service is entirely legitimate. Cultivating love for the neighbor, especially the neighbor who is not personally attractive to us, is a direct fulfillment of Jesus' teaching. Indeed, understanding that these nontheistic spiritualities enable us to respond better to God's call may deepen our appreciation for them.

The fact that there are so many spiritualities—including many I have not mentioned—should free us to pursue those that we find truly helpful and at the same time free us from any sense of requirement to pursue any spiritual discipline. We are justified by faith, not by practices. There is always a danger that practices be treated as law. People who find a practice helpful sometimes try to impose it on others. Others feel guilty because they do not have a regular discipline. Faith frees us to practice a spiritual discipline. It also frees us not to practice any. For me, one great strength of Whitehead's philosophy is that so many diverse types of experience can be explained by it. That means that we can learn much about reality as a whole and about ourselves from practitioners of all these disciplines. We can be grateful for their multiplicity and that we now live in a world in which we can be appreciatively aware of this multiplicity.

If I am then asked what kind of spirituality a process theologian favors, I find it hard to answer. I suppose the answer will be: the one that most helps you to love and serve God and creatures. If you need no special discipline in order to do that effectively, you are still quite free to explore and experiment. You are also free to live the life of love and service, trusting in God, without special disciplines.

TWO

Pathways to Spiritual Transformation

Bruce G. Epperly

PROCESS THEOLOGY affirms that reality is complex, multi-faceted, dynamic, and interdependent in nature. Although each moment of experience is unique and unrepeatable, the whole universe conspires to birth each momentary experience, whether it is at the cellular, organic, animal, emotional, intellectual, or spiritual levels of experience. In process thought, there are no clearly defined physical, emotional, intellectual, or spiritual compartments. All aspects of life are interrelated, constantly shaping and being shaped by one another.

Process theology and spirituality take the traditional doctrines of divine omnipresence, omniscience, and omni-activity seriously, even as they reinterpret them in terms of relationship, transformation, and partnership.[1] To the process theologian, these are not abstract doctrines, but concrete aspects of every creaturely experience.

Spiritual formation calls us to experience "lived omnipresence." With the German mystic Meister Eckhart, process spirituality affirms that "all things are words of God." All creatures, including ourselves, have direct, although mostly unconscious, encounters with the Holy Adventure. Furthermore, God's presence is lively, dynamic, creative, and contextual. God's desire for beauty, love, and wholeness, is embodied uniquely in each concrete moment of experience. Accordingly, process theology and spirituality assert that there is no ideal, or all-encompassing, spiritual path. God's personal relationship with each moment of experience is reflected in God's unique desire for each person at each moment and season of her or his life. While God's desire for wholeness is gentle and noncoercive, it may burst forth in life-changing and miraculous ways when the divine and human spirits are in spiritual alignment. In her book *The Secret Life of Bees,* Sue Monk Kidd describes the ubiquitous activity of divine wisdom in an exchange between wise woman August and young Lily:

> Her spirit is everywhere, Lily, just everywhere. In rocks and trees and even people, but sometimes it will get concentrated in certain places, and just beam out at you in a special way.[2]

God's desire for wholeness and beauty is balanced with God's embrace of all creation in God's own evolving experience of the universe. God is truly the "One to whom all hearts are open and all desires known." Creative and receptive love are woven together in the intimacy of God's relationship with the world. The omnipresent God hears our prayers, feels our pain, and experiences the deepest desires of our hearts. The One who brings forth each moment of experience with a holy vision also receives and treasures each moment of experience forevermore.

While there is no *one* spiritual path or understanding of ultimate reality, life-transforming spiritual experience is grounded in the interplay of three practical affirmations:

1. We can articulate our experience of God and the world in an inspiring and rational vision, or theological world view.
2. We can experience the God about whom we speak.
3. We can formulate spiritual practices that enable us to experience more fully the vision of God and the world that we affirm.

In other words, process spiritual formation presents a *vision*, a *promise*, and a *path* to experiencing the divine.

As John Cobb notes, there are "multiple spiritualities," or multiple paths, to experiencing God's presence in our lives. In a sense, these multiple spiritual paths correspond to the Hindu notion of "yogas" or ways to the divine, based on one's personality and spiritual orientation, and the image of "stages of life" from youth to old age, suggested by Hindu sages as well as American psychologists such as Erik Erikson, James Fowler, and Carol Gilligan.

If all things are reflections of God's intimate and personal presence, then God has many reflections within the world, each one of which finds its fulfillment through specific spiritual paths. While the list is not exhaustive, God's unique presence is mediated through and shaped by factors such as age, race, ethnicity, nationality, economics, religious background, gender and sexual identity, family of origin, and health condition. Further, our Myers-Briggs personality type, enneagram number, or dominant way of approaching the world in terms of "multiple intelligences" both limits and shapes our concrete experience of God and the spiritual practices that support our relationship with God. In a pluralistic universe, we must avoid advocating one spiritual path for all persons. Accordingly, in each chapter, I will suggest certain spiritual practices and emphases that emerge from the insights of process theology and spirituality. My goal will be to complement John Cobb's theological reflections with spiritual practices appropriate to process thought. In this chapter, I will focus on the paths of embodiment and healing energy.

The Path of Embodiment

John Cobb notes that spiritualities that emphasize the body make "good sense for a Whiteheadian, since the integrated flow of experience that we think of as ourselves derives most of its content from events in the body. To change the body is to change experience. To achieve a relaxed and harmonious bodily condition enables the body to contribute to the well-being of the psyche and even to the attainment of certain psychic states." In a world of dynamic relationships, mind and body flow into one another seamlessly. Spirit is embodied and the body is inspired. Healing the body or reframing painful somatic experiences can contribute to the healing of mind, emotions, and spirit. Spiritual transformation can transform the body and bring about not only a reduction in stress and alleviation of pain, but also gradual physical healing and, in rare instances, physical cures. I must add however that even spiritual healing is not isolated from other environmental and personal factors. In my experience as a spiritual guide, energy worker, and healing minister, most persons who experience profound physical transformation through the laying of hands, anointing with oil, spiritual affirmations, meditative practices, or intercessory prayer are also receiving complementary or technological medical care and the loving care of a community of friends.[3]

Historically, the body has often been forgotten, denied, or abused by persons in search of the holy. In contrast, Whiteheadian spirituality is wholly/holy embodied. God is experienced as fully in touch and in movement as in quiet contemplation and theological reflection. God is the Spirit of the universe, whose relationship to the world is similar to the interdependent relationship of our own minds and bodies. Accordingly, it is important for us to develop spiritual practices that nurture our experience of holy embodiment.

Wholly breathing. It has been said that spirituality aims at enabling persons to do ordinary things in extraordinary ways. As the Zen saying asserts, "before enlightenment, I chopped wood and carried water, and after enlightenment, I chopped wood and carried water." One of the most fundamental activities and precise barometers of our well-being is our breathing. Nothing is more ordinary, or more revealing of our spiritual state. When we are anxious, our breath is often shallow and quick. On the other hand, when we are confident and at peace, our breath is regular and deep. We can transform our state of mind simply by taking a moment to be still and breathe slowly and deeply.

Psalm 150 proclaims, "let everything that lives praise [God]!" The breath of God permeates the universe, giving life and energy to all things, human and nonhuman. If we are intentional in our breathing, each breath may connect us with God and our human and nonhuman companions on the planet. Our breathing can be a vehicle for spiritual awareness, prayerful intercession, or gentle calming.

In the 1970s, spiritual guide Alan Armstrong Hunter taught a very simple breath prayer to Claremont graduate and seminary students such as my wife Kate and myself. With every inhalation, we were asked to imagine that we were breathing in God's healing and centering breath as we quietly affirmed, "I breathe the Spirit deeply in." As we exhaled, we breathed our particular emotional or spiritual state into God's care. Today, many Christians have been influenced by a similar practice, taught by Vietnamese Buddhist monk Thich Naht Hahn who counsels, "breathing in

I feel calm, breathing out I smile." Every breath is a holy breath, a healing breath, a centering and calming breath. To this day, I take a few centering breaths before each class session, as I shuffle my sermon notes at the pulpit, or as I prepare to enter a hospital room or conflict situation. In addition, I take time for centering and calming breath when I become aware that I am becoming anxious or experiencing the stress of balancing my administrative, teaching, and pastoral responsibilities at the seminary with my family life. In that centering breath, I experience God's deep peace breathing in and with me, inviting me to experience life as spacious and abundant rather than constricted and impoverished. Imaginatively, I experience myself breathing the energy of the birth of the universe and the healing power of Jesus of Nazareth with each inhalation andsending forth healing energy to the world as I exhale.

> *Take a moment and simply breathe. Exhale all the stress of your life. Inhale deeply and slowly, breathing from your stomach, experience God's spirit entering your whole being. Feel the spirit energizing every cell and organ and bringing lively and creative energy to your brain. Feel the stress disappear as you exhale. Experience yourself as breathing with the One "in whom you live, move, and have your being." (Acts 17:28)*

Breath prayer can be done anywhere. You may choose to breathe gently for twenty minutes as part of your morning meditation. You may also take a moment for wholly/holy breathing as you answer the phone, greet a friend, or as you begin to feel yourself overwhelmed by the first waves of stress on a busy day. In wholly/holy breathing, you will discover that peace and wholeness can be found in any situation.

In each moment, we can breathe in concert with the ever-lively and ever-present Spirit of God. As we quietly align our own breathing with the universal breath of the Spirit, we may experience God's guidance through God's constantly inspiring "sighs too deep for words" (Romans 8:26).

Moving in the Spirit. In the film *Chariots of Fire,* runner Eric Liddell proclaims, "God made me fast, and when I run I can feel God's pleasure." A dynamic universe invites us to move in synch with the lively and adventurous Spirit of God. We may move in concert with God's Spirit through yoga postures, T'ai Chi, ritualized body prayers, or simply by exercising aerobically in a contemplative and compassionate spirit. In this section, I describe four very simple body prayers that join movement and contemplation.

Process theologian Patricia Adams Farmer invites persons to take a "beauty break" in the course of each day. A spiritual beauty break awakens our senses to the wonder of life and the divine presence bursting forth in all things. While a beauty break can take many forms, I suggest a "beauty walk" for persons who wish to integrate spiritual formation with their regular exercise routines. In the practice of beauty walking, you may begin your walk with a quiet meditative moment, awakening your senses to God's beauty and giving thanks for the wonder of your life and the universe. Let go of the demands and anxieties of the past and the projects of the future. Feel the holiness of your body, as you breathe deeply, from head to toe.

> *As you begin your walk, simply open your eyes, bathing your senses in the multi-colored, many faceted world. Feel the breeze in its stillness or gusts. Experience your embodiment as you walk in awareness. Experience your connectedness with all things, human and nonhuman. If your mind wanders, bring it back to the present experience of what Rabbi Abraham*

Joshua Heschel described as "radical amazement." Conclude your walk with a prayer of thanksgiving for the beauty of life and a prayer of commitment that you may live appreciatively and act lovingly to preserve this beautiful Earth.

In a variation on this theme, another walking—or running, swimming, or biking—prayer simply joins movement with breathing. As I walk, I simply breathe deeply God's Spirit, noting my inhaling and exhaling, or praying an affirmation such as "I breathe the Spirit deeply in" or "Breathing in I feel calm, breathing out I smile."

Walking prayer can also integrate spiritual affirmations with opening to God's ever-present energy. In the following paragraph, I describe one of my regular spiritual practices.

I begin my walk with the affirmation "this is the day that God has made, I will rejoice and be glad in it." After I have found my appropriate walking speed, I begin to notice my breath as I breathe gently and deeply. I begin to focus my breath, experiencing God's divine healing, energy, and power, filling my body, mind, spirit, and emotions with each breath. In a fashion similar to the energy centers of traditional Chinese medicine or the chakras of Hindu metaphysics, I focus this healing breath on the top of the head (divine wisdom), the head (intellectual clarity and integrity), the throat (immune system functioning), the heart (circulatory and respiratory systems), the solar plexus (digestive system), the genitals (reproductive system), and the anus (eliminative system). While each of these energy centers has a physical focus, each one also corresponds to a spiritual/emotional state. I experience God's wholeness supporting my own well-being in body mind and spirit.

After I have grounded myself in the soles of my feet, I follow the same pattern, now going upward from one spiritual center to the other. However, on the upward journey, I combine prayers and affirmations with my breathing. At the anus, I affirm "I let go and let God" and take a moment to forgive any persons with whom I have grievances. At the second center, the genitals, I affirm as I breathe, "Divine creativity and intimacy" as I pray for my creative projects.

At the solar plexus, I breathe in "divine energy and power" as I affirm "I can do all things with Christ who strengthens me" and experience God's light flooding every cell in my body. At the heart, I affirm "divine love and courage" as I pray for friends, family, and world situations and experience divine power surging with each breath and heartbeat. At the throat, I affirm "God's healing words" as I pray "let the words of my mouth and the meditation of my heart be acceptable to you, O Lord, my rock and my redeemer." At this point, I let God's healing breath permeate and energize my immune system. As I breathe God's healing and enlightening energy into my forehead ("third eye"), I affirm that "I align myself with divine intelligence and order" and experience God's abundance, energy, creativity, and prosperity flowing through my life toward the world. I see myself as a channel of God's love and wholeness to the world. As I breathe through the top of my head, I affirm that "God's wisdom is guiding me in all the events of my life." I conclude this process by experiencing God's empowering and healing breath permeating my whole being and surrounding my body in a way that both welcomes and protects.

This meditative prayer joins East and West, meditation and movement, and body and mind in its alignment of the practitioner with God's Holy Energy.

Praying the body. Yoga, Qi Gong, and T'ai Chi seek to connect our bodies with the energy of the universe. When the energy of the universe harmoniously flows through us without obstruction, we experience wholeness and vitality. When the divine energy is disordered or blocked, we experience disease and fatigue. Process theology affirms the energetic nature of reality and recognizes that our embodiment of divine energy can be dynamic or sluggish, in synch or chaotic.

Historically, Christians have also employed body postures as part of their prayer lives. While these postures have not explicitly been used to promote physical well-being, the alignment of humans with God and one another promotes wholeness of body, mind, and spirit.

Many Christians have joined body prayer or spiritual postures with chanting hymns from the Taizé community in France or while doing sacred dance. Simple movements place our bodies in the divine center and align our breathing with the breath of God that enlivens and guides.

A prayer that has been especially meaningful to the spiritual adventures of my wife Kate and myself involves slowly singing a chant we learned at the Shalem Institute for Spiritual Formation in Washington, D.C.[4] The simple chant involves repeating the words, "I thank you God for the wonder of my being." The body movements are equally simple.

> *Beginning in a comfortable standing posture, bend over gently as if you are planning to touch our toes. As you begin to chant, "I thank you God," raise your body slowly to an upright position and raise your arms slowly to a place over your head, with your hands and arms wide open in a position of prayer and praise. As you sing, "for the wonder of my being," lower your arms and fold them over your heart.*

This chant affirms the goodness of a God-created life and the wonder and beauty of our own lives as God's beloved daughters and sons, the embodiments of God's holy desire for beauty and creativity. We can also sing this chant to affirm God's presence and beauty in others: "I thank you God for the wonder of *all* being" or "I thank you God for the wonder of *(person's name)* being."

In our awareness of the unfolding and intricate interplay of the divine adventure and human creativity, we discover that all places, including our own bodies, are holy and beautiful.

Healing Spirituality

The final lines of W. H. Auden's Advent Oratorio, *For the Time Being*, challenge followers of Jesus to "love [God] in the world of the flesh." While fasting and simplicity of life may be appropriate spiritual practices for certain persons, process theology proclaims that God is fully present and may be experienced in the concrete realities of embodied existence. Spirit permeates and enlivens flesh and intellect alike. God is revealed in a mother's womb as well as in a theologian's reflections. Ironically, just as theologians are rediscovering the body as a vehicle for divine revelation, physicians and scientists are also exploring the role of spiritual practices, religious commitment, and intercessory prayer in overall physical well-being. Medical studies and personal experience reveal that physical well-being contributes to emotional and spiritual wholeness. These studies also affirm that spiritual transformation may also contribute to overall physical well-being.

Faithful touch. Healing spirituality takes many forms, both liturgical and non-liturgical. On the one hand, traditional Christian practices such as anointing with oil and laying on of hands focus and mediate God's healing power within a community of faith. Faithful communities enable persons to respond creatively to illness and bereavement; they may also support persons' quests for physical and spiritual healing. Intercessory prayer radiates across the universe, creating a healing field of force around those for whom we pray. In an interdependent world, our prayers truly make a difference to those for whom we pray as well as to God. Prayer positively transforms the environment and, thus, supports God's intimate desire for wholeness of body, mind, and spirit. As Marjorie Suchocki asserts,

> Intercessory praying changes what the world is relative to the one for whom we pray, and that change is for the good. This relational theology indicates that we become one with those for whom we pray within God's own being, for we meet in God. It is God who feels this man's condition; it is God who feels my own condition in praying for him; it is God who weaves me into the man's welfare.[5]

Laying on of hands and anointing with oil create a healing field that inspires hope and transformation in the cells of our bodies as well as our minds. As we touch others in faith, we receive and shape the healing energy that was present in the ministry of Jesus of Nazareth.

Healing energy. Whitehead's metaphysics portrays the world in terms of lively, dynamic, interdependent, and energetic drops of experience. Divine energy permeates and gives life to all things, from liver cells to the imagination. Whether through liturgical laying on of hands or the work of energy workers, God's universal energy is focused, enlivened, and balanced to promote the healing of body, mind, and spirit. Cobb notes the metaphysical basis for the mutual transformation of mind and body:

> Bodily events are just as real as psychic events. But just as bodily events profoundly influence psychic ones, so also psychic events profoundly influence bodily ones.

Many Christians mediate God's energy through hands-on practices such as reiki (universal energy), healing touch, and therapeutic touch.[6] While each of these healing practices has as its primary focus the body, the energy that transforms, balances, and revitalizes the body equally transforms the mind and spirit. As mysterious as the laying on of hands and anointing with oil, these practices create a sacred place within which God's healing energy flows more abundantly. In my experience in congregational as well as complementary healing ministries, I have found that healing touch not only knits together broken bones but also broken hearts. It awakens us to new energy as well as creative and innovative ideas. God's aim at healing and wholeness in our relationships, body, and spirit, moves through the media of touch as well as meditation. In a time in which many persons experience the destructive psychological and spiritual impact of inappropriate and abusive touch in the context of families and religious institutions, healing touch enables us to reclaim God's presence and beauty in our constantly changing physical bodies.

Process thought proclaims that all things are centers of experience. Accordingly, the body contains both positive and negative memories of previous experiences. The spiritual focus of any healing touch activates the divine movement toward wholeness, beauty, and peace. When we touch others with love, our touch is prayerful and healing. The integration of healing touch with body prayers and other spiritual disciplines, along with appropriate psychotherapy, weaves together the transformation of physical memory, emotional and mental health, and spiritual life. The omni-active, omnipresent, and omniscient God permeates every cell and every event with the aim that we experience life in all its abundance.

Notes

1. I prefer the word "omni-activity" to "omnipotence" because it affirms that although God is constantly creating and sustaining the universe and moving within each moment of experience, God's power, presence, and passion works within the conditioned freedom of the world. God creates within all things, even though God does not determine all things.
2. Sue Monk Kidd, *The Secret Life of Bees* (New York: Penguin Books, 2002), 141.
3. For more on spirituality, embodiment, and healing see Bruce Epperly *At the Edges of Life* (St. Louis: Chalice, 1992); *Spirituality and Health, Health and Spirituality* (Mystic, CT: Twenty-third Publications, 1997); *God's Touch: Faith, Wholeness, and the Healing Miracles of Jesus* (Louisville: Westminster/John Knox, 2001); *Walking in the Light: Christian and Jewish Perspectives on Spirituality and Health,* written with Lewis Solomon (St. Louis: Chalice, 2004).
4. For more information on the Shalem Institute, see their web site www. shalem.org.
5. Marjorie Suchocki, *In God's Presence* (St. Louis: Chalice Press, 1996), p. 46–47.
6. For more on the relationship of Christian spirituality to these forms of healing touch, see Bruce Epperly, *Cross and Crystal: Christianity and the New Age in Creative Dialogue* (Mystic, CT: Twenty-third Publications, 1996), *God's Touch: Faith, Whole- ness, and the Healing Miracles of Jesus* (Louisville: Westminster/John Knox, 2001), and *Reiki Healing Touch and the Way of Jesus* (Kelowna, B.C., Canada: Northstone Press, 2005).

THREE

Communal Spiritual Practice in Ceremony and Liturgy

Paul S. Nancarrow

Process theology is able to affirm the value of many sorts of spiritual practices, derived from many sorts of religious traditions. In Chapter One, especially, John Cobb provides a Whiteheadian reading of spiritual practices found in Buddhist, Hindu, Native American, Jungian, and Christian traditions. He emphasizes that, from a Whiteheadian point of view, there is value in practices that raise awareness of reality as it is, that reduce attachments to the sense of a substantial self, that encourage imaginative empathy with others (including nonhuman others), that promote discernment of God's aims in our experience, and that increase our compassionate service to others. Of special interest are spiritual practices that promote a more integrated and holistic relationship between body and psyche. Likewise, Bruce Epperly in the previous chapter emphasizes "the path of embodiment" as a major theme in a process spirituality's pathways to spiritual transformation.

Yet another feature of a process approach to spiritual practice is an emphasis on the importance of *community* in any spiritual path. We often think of spirituality as something practiced in solitude; indeed, Cobb criticizes the individualism and consumerism lurking within what passes for spirituality in many contemporary accounts. Process thought, however, emphasizes the importance of *society* in all real experience. Everything we encounter in the world around us is a society: enduring things like chairs, trees, books, persons, our own sense of self and spirit, are all *societies of occasions*, moments of fleeting experience grouped together by common themes and streams of influence. Process thought stresses than nothing happens in a vacuum, but all moments of experience arise in and contribute to wider societies and societies of societies. Our moments of spiritual experience arise within the societies of our bodies; our moments of personal experience arise within the societies of our families and communities and interpersonal relationships; our moments of intensely private experience arise within our social circles of public commitments and global involvements. A process spirituality must take account of the social dimension of spiritual practice.

These two particular emphases of process spirituality—embodiment and society—come together in the practices of ritual, ceremony, and liturgy as spiritual paths. To many, the idea of "ritual spirituality" may seem at first like an oxymoron, a contradiction in terms. To many people today, ritual belongs to the sphere of the "religious," as in the phrase "I'm spiritual, not religious." To many people today, group ceremonies and church liturgies seem archaic and outdated; indeed, as Cobb points out, part of the reason for the resurgence of interest in spirituality among Protestants today is the fact that forms of congregational worship, often dominated by the "wordiness" of Bible reading and preaching, have largely ceased to meet worshipers' spiritual needs. But a process approach to spirituality can help us take a fresh look at ritual and liturgy, and to see in them positive values of embodiment and society. Ritual action involves the body: there are gestures to be made, postures to be adopted, symbolic objects to be handled, colors to be seen, incenses to be smelled, foods to be tasted. Liturgical action involves the community: there are prayers to be recited together, songs to be harmonized, greetings and dialogues to be spoken to each other, touches to be exchanged, faces and voices and needs other than one's own to be encountered. A process approach to liturgy can help to revitalize our appreciation of ritual and ceremony as genuinely *spiritual* practices. This is true for all religious traditions, but may be especially important for American Protestantism in this current atmosphere of spiritual interest.

In the process approach, part of the power to revitalize liturgy lies in its ability to focus attention on the actual *doing* of liturgy in faithful communities. Often, when we hear or use the word "liturgy," what comes to mind is a *text*, a series of prayers and scripture readings and hymns laid out in a certain sequence, an order of service that can be printed on a page and handed out to worshipers or published in a newsletter. But a process approach, with its emphasis on actuality and occasions, reminds us that a liturgy is not just a form of words or a sequence of texts, but is first and foremost a prayerful *action*, a faithful *happening*, a thing that is *done*. Just as a playscript is not fully realized until it is acted, or a symphony score isn't really music until it is performed, so a liturgy isn't all it is meant to be until it is *prayed*. The liturgy of Baptism, for instance, doesn't just talk about washing from sin or anointing with the Holy Spirit, but splashes in water and pours on oil; the liturgy of Eucharist doesn't just set apart bread and wine to gaze at as symbols of the presence of Christ, but breaks the bread and pours out the wine and feeds the worshipers with tangible, tastable food. The reality of liturgy is in the *doing*—and this is something that a process spirituality helps us to speak about with greater clarity and insight. The process approach invites us to look at what a ritual *does*, and how it does it, and how its influence flows into an actual experience of prayer in the always-and-everywhere presence of God.

In process terms, rituals and ceremonies can be considered as *propositions*, "lures for feeling." Liturgies set forth possibilities for dynamic relationships between people and significant objects and God, relationships that would not exist, or would not be as accessible, in the ordinary course of worldly affairs. The flow of action from one moment to another in a ritual celebration lures worshipers' feelings toward certain kinds of combinations—connections of thoughts, emotions, memories, and intentions that produce an intensity and harmony of experience that an old Anglican prayer calls "the beauty of holiness." That feeling of beauty evoked by liturgy can, in its turn, open into a feeling of the love and the call of God present in the worshipers' own individual and shared circumstances.

Consider, for example, what happens in the liturgical gesture of passing the peace, which is part of the eucharistic rites of many Christian communities. The presider says, "The peace of Christ be always with you." On one level this is a personal greeting from one member of the community to the rest of the community, with all the personal affection and goodwill inherent in such a greeting; on another level, it is a deliberate echo of the greeting the Risen Christ gave to his disciples in the upper room (see Luke 24:36, John 20:19), and so carries with it all the resonance of the promise of new life in peace with God given in the paschal mystery. As each congregant turns to a neighbor and repeats, "Peace be with you," new layers of personal feeling and relevance are added: friends who haven't seen each other since last week are glad to speak, two who have been in conflict or working through a misunderstanding act out a new commitment to reconciliation, one who knows another is in pain or sorrow shares a deep prayer for well-being in saying the simple word "Peace." Each handshake or hug is a unique encounter and sharing of feelings; yet all are taken up into the wider field of meaning of the promise of peace in Christ. The presence of the love of Jesus permeates the entire ritual exchange, as each worshiper recalls and reenacts Jesus' peacemaking love in her or his own ceremonial greetings. By offering Christ's resurrection greeting as a model or lure for feeling, the liturgical action embodies the possibility for participants to enter into divinely graced relationships of peace and promise that would be obscured, hurried over, even impossible, in the ordinary rush of social experience.

This sort of richness of actual experience goes far beyond what we might expect from looking at the mere text, "The peace of Christ be always with you. / And also with you!" The fullness of gesture, the subtext of feeling, the presence of memory, the solidity of physical contact, the signification of language, the aspiration to peace—all come together in the flow of action to give the occasion a depth and weight and importance far greater than words and images alone. By focusing on the gesture as something *acted*, something acted in the body and acted in the community, process spirituality helps reclaim ritual gesture as a genuine spiritual practice.

A process spirituality of liturgical practice draws our attention to our embodied social involvements. It can also help us attend to our *ultimate* social involvement, our society with God, the primordial relationality in which all things live and move and have their being. Ritual practice can help reconnect our actions to God's fundamental aims for the universe.

This is because liturgy may be said to happen on at least two levels: a human level, and a divine level. Liturgies are occasions (or, more technically, societies of occasions) taking place in the corporate lives of religious communities, and in the personal lives of their individual members; liturgies are also occasions in the life of God. This is especially important for Christian liturgies that are also identified as sacraments, because in these liturgies the human activities of ceremony and ritual are held to be outward and visible signs of inward and spiritual grace, human signs by which God actively effects divine ends. But I think it can be claimed of all liturgy, indeed of all prayer, that it is simultaneously a human act and a divine act, a moment in the lives of people and a moment in the life of God. Liturgy, then, partakes of divine purposes. Liturgy enacts God's purpose on a human scale and in a human context and in a human way.

In very general terms, we can say that God's purpose in the world is the evocation of ever-richer forms of experience. "The teleology of the Universe," Whitehead writes, "is directed to the production of Beauty," where "Beauty" is maximum intensity of feeling with maximum harmony of feeling.[1] Such Beauty is a feature of God's own experience of the world: as God receives into Godself the multifarious occasions of the Universe, God feels each moment with its own intensity, and God also feels the moments in their togetherness, God feels the moments as they are harmonized in God's own all-embracing perspective. Beauty, richness of experience, is first of all a quality of God.

But God does not, as it were, hoard this Beauty as a private possession: God wishes to share richness of experience with the creatures, and so God gives each new moment of creaturely experience an aim that it, also, realize a maximum intensity of feeling with maximum harmony of feeling. God's purpose for each particular occasion is that it reflects God's own richness of experience to the extent and to the degree and in the scope that it is able.

So the *particular* features of the initial aims God gives to creaturely moments differ as to the capacity of the creature, yet all God's aims for creatures share the *general* characteristic of striving for richness of experience. And all realizations of richness of experience, all accomplishments of creaturely Beauty, of whatever size and scope, reenter into God and become components in God's experience of Beauty in the Universe. Thus God not only *perceives* the Universe as Beautiful, but God lures and woos the Universe into *becoming* more Beautiful.

Liturgy is one stream of influence by which that wooing-into-Beauty takes shape in human life within the Universe. Cobb notes in Chapter One that all occasions of human experience begin with a God-given aim, but that the divine origin of such aims is typically buried in the influx of the data of experience, and we are not generally conscious of God's aims for us in the immediacies of our experiences. On some occasions, however, God's aims for us might include the specific element that we be *aware* of God's presence and activity, that our experience be, frankly, *religious* experience. Experiences of prayer, meditation, scripture study, or ceremony might embody aims from God that we be especially aware of an intimacy with God, or a judgment of God, or a call of God, or co-creative communion with God; such awareness brings a with it a particular richness of experience, a particular intensity and harmony, that makes these moments peculiarly reflective of God's purposes. In such moments we can live in a more intense way our vocation to be created co-creators with God, making Beauty for our world and for God.

Because liturgy is corporate and communal spirituality, liturgy brings a social dimension to the realization of Beauty in accordance with God's purposes. A liturgical ceremony is a society of occasions in which streams of influence from God, from the corporate history of the community, from the individual life-stories of the worshipers, and from the material conditions of the present world, are all woven together in a rich experience of grace and empowerment. My own prayer is made more vivid, more intense, and more harmonious, in being joined together with the prayer of others in the tradition of a community. In a liturgy of intercession, for instance, I might be aware of my prayer for a sick friend; but when I hear spoken out loud one person's prayer for her friend, and another person's prayer for his family, and another person's prayer for a nation decimated by war, and I am aware that my prayer is joined with all these other prayers in a shared yearning for compassion and action, then my experience of prayer is made the richer, the more intense and more harmonious, the more Beautiful, for that liturgical sharing. Or when I preside at a celebration of the Eucharist, as presider it is my role to speak the Eucharistic Prayer on behalf of the whole assembly; but when I have heard others read scriptures, and sing hymns, and preach a sermon, and offer intercessions and thanksgivings, then my speaking of the Eucharistic Prayer is deepened and intensified by the awareness of sharing prayer with all these others—and as my speaking of the prayer becomes more vivid because of my intense feelings, it evokes more intense prayerful feelings from the others as well. In liturgy the varied gifts and roles and offerings of many are brought together into a single corporate act of prayer that is richer, more intense, and more harmonious, more charged with the Beauty of the purpose of God, than the prayers of the many would be on their own.

Liturgical celebrations, then, are both means and ends in God's work to accomplish the purpose of Beauty in the Universe.

A well-formed, well-prayed liturgy is a moment of Beauty, an accomplished fact of rich experience for all its participants. As such, it adds to the total amount of Beauty in the Universe and passes into God to be felt by God as a component in the total Beauty of all that is. Each liturgy is an end in itself, a realization of a particular intense harmony and harmonious intensity in a particular context. But each liturgy is also a means, a lure to a greater feeling of Beauty in a greater and more inclusive context. Every liturgy reveals God's ultimate purpose in the Universe: because every liturgy is a gathering of many elements into one harmonious intensity, every liturgy is a picture "in miniature" of what God wants for the universe as a whole. Each accomplished liturgy is, therefore, not just an isolated fact of Beauty, but a fact of Beauty that points beyond itself to the possibility of yet greater accomplishments of Beauty in societies of occasions that draw together more diverse elements into more intense harmonies. As with Isaiah, whose liturgy of burning incense in the Temple opened up into an experience of the liturgy of heaven around God's throne, and issued in a call to be God's prophet and bear God's word to the people (Isaiah 6:1-8)—so with us, whose liturgies give us experiences of Beauty that open up into yearning for the yet greater Beauty of inclusive well-being for all God's creatures, and issue into the call to us to be co-creators with God of well-being in every way we can. Liturgy is an accomplishment of God's purpose, and also a revelation of God's greater purpose, in rite and ceremony and corporate prayer.

So liturgy enacts God's purpose on two levels: on the divine level, it accomplishes Beauty that God can feel and harmonize into God's experience of the universe as one; and on the human level, it incorporates us into the realizing of God's aims for Beauty, for richness of experience, for inclusive well-being, as created co-creators and on behalf of all God's creatures. A process spirituality of liturgical practice will be aware of this multilayered reality of ritual and will help worshipers participate more fully in the work of the Beauty of holiness.

How then can a process spirituality translate these reflections on ritual and liturgy into actual spiritual practices? The answers will be varied, inasmuch as actual liturgical practices vary from tradition to tradition and community to community. Worship styles, liturgical texts and songs, ceremonial gestures are very different in Baptist, Methodist, Pentecostal, Roman Catholic, megachurch, Episcopal, Eastern Orthodox settings—not to mention differences between church, synagogue, mosque, temple, and meditation center. What process spirituality can bring to liturgy is not necessarily a new set of practices, but a new *way* of practicing; what process spirituality can bring to liturgy is a new *quality* of acting the traditional ritual actions.

With that in mind, I suggest the following very general qualities of acting that can be exemplified in a process spirituality of liturgical practice. These suggestions are derived mostly from my own experience of worship in the Episcopal tradition with its *Book of Common Prayer*; but they will offer points of contact with any tradition that gathers for some form of public worship.

Be Attentive

One of the things that can make traditional liturgies seem dull and unengaging is that we only attend to them with a small portion of our minds and hearts. Simply *paying attention* to the embodied, communal dimensions of a liturgical gathering can bring a new sense of life, movement, and God's presence to the ceremonial proceedings.

- *Locate yourself in the worship space.* Before the service begins, find a place in a pew or chair; sit down; take a deep breath or two; allow yourself to become centered. Feel the surface on which you sit, the weight or lightness of your body; the air you breathe. Let thoughts of where you came from or how you got here fade into the background; let anticipations of where you'll be going or what you'll be doing after the service claim less of your attention; be *here* and *now* in the place of prayer.

- *Feast your eyes on the worship space.* Look around and savor what you see. What kind of architecture does the nave or sanctuary have? Are there carvings or statues or icons or stained-glass windows? Is there an altar or table, a pulpit, a baptismal font?—how are they arranged relative to each other? Are there other forms of special liturgical furniture— a bema, an ark, an incense burner, a Buddha figure? Are there colored hangings on the altar, banners on the walls, seasonal decorations around the room? Are symbols worked into the decorations or adornments?—do you know what the symbols mean? Are there flowers or greenery or live plants in the sanctuary? If the worship space is very spare and unadorned, how does its spareness make you feel? How does the room enclose and shape the space? What is the room's geometry? How does the presence of people in the room change and define the space it encloses? Be attentive to whatever is there to be seen and let yourself feel each item as helping to constitute the environment that now harbors your own vivid embodiment.

- *Attend to your other senses as well.* While many Christian worship spaces are designed primarily around the visual sense, there may be other sensory cues in the space as well. One seminary chapel in Wisconsin I visited as a child will always be anchored in my memory by the smell of beeswax candles and incense. What do you smell in this worship space? What do you hear?—an organ prelude, people shuffling papers, conversations in the entryway, musicians tuning up, traffic noises from outside, a deep stillness, slight echoes from a gothic ceiling high above? What do you feel?—beneath the presented immediacies of the senses are causal efficacies of emotion, association, motivation, longing, hope, joy. What nonsensory depths do the sensory cues of the worship space trigger in you? The data of perceptions other than sight also contribute to our awareness of being embodied in a particular environment, and also constitute the social context of our ritual practice.

- *Observe the people around you.* Who is sharing this space with you? Before the service begins, don't be afraid to engage in a little "spiritual people-watching." You may recognize faces; you may be very close friends with many of the people in attendance; you may be among strangers. As you notice who is with you, remember that each of them is a subject, each brings his or her own needs and gifts and concerns and baggage and aspirations to this liturgy. As the service progresses, be attentive to how people move, how they sound, how they participate; one may offer a particular prayer during the intercessions, one may sing a favorite hymn with an evident emotion of enjoyment, one may seem silent and withdrawn and yet has clearly made the effort to bring his or her private prayers to this public place. Look at the people around you and be mindful of the relationships you share, especially the relationships created and embodied in this very liturgical action. As a child, I was taught that it is not polite to stare at people in church; but I think now that *paying attention* to people in church is not only a matter of courtesy, it is a practice of building up communion in the social environment of prayer.

Participate Fully

Someone once said that "worship is not a spectator sport." At its best, liturgy invites the involvement of *all* the people present, not only those with particular roles to play "up front," but also the whole gathered assembly. To be sure, there have been times in the history of the church where liturgy has devolved into a ceremonial performance by religious professionals before a passive congregational audience; I'm sure the same could be said in other religious traditions as well. But the liturgy is intended to be "the work of the people," in which all those present are able to participate.[2] In order for ritual action to be a genuinely spiritual practice, it must be undertaken with the fullest degree of participation we can muster.

- *Join in the congregational passages.* In most liturgical celebrations there are passages which the congregation reads or recites in a single massed voice, such as the Lord's Prayer, the Creed or Affirmation of Belief, the Confession of Sin, or the Prayer of the Day. These traditional texts offer a lure for your personal devotional feeling; but they also provide the matrix of a social occasion that can take up your feeling into a larger feeling of solidarity and communion with the assembly before God. Use your full voice to speak the passage aloud, attending to the meaning of the words and bringing your own interpretive understanding to the reading. At the same time, listen to the voices that join with you in the passage; listen for *their* vocal qualities and the way their reading expresses *their* understanding. Be mindful that the passage is a multilayered and polysemous reality, and that your own participation makes it that much more vital and alive.

- *Speak the responses.* In many Christian traditions, there is a great deal of dialogue in liturgical worship. The presider may greet the people "God be with you," and the people respond "And also with you"; intercessory litanies may call for regular responses, such as when the leader says "God, in your mercy," and the people respond "Hear our prayer"; the presider may invite the people to thanksgiving, saying "Lift up your hearts," and the people respond "We lift them to the Lord." Sometimes prayers are said responsively, songs are sung as call-and-response, psalms are recited antiphonally. Although they may be brief and are often highly stylized, these bits of dialogue in the service are meant to be real moments of exchange, when the assembly acts as a social unit transcending and including the individual worshipers. When you make the responses, speak them in a strong and clear voice. Let the words gather and express your own feeling of being a fully participant member of the assembly.

- *Move.* Many forms of worship service include some kind of movements and gestures. They may be as simple as standing to sing, or making the sign of the cross, or clasping hands to pray; they may be as elaborate as liturgical dance, or processions to and from the altar for communion, or lengthy exchanges of hugs and handshakes at the passing of the peace. Not all congregations make the same gestures, and not all members of an assembly will join in every movement. In my own congregation, some cross themselves at the final blessing, and some do not; it is a matter of personal piety and preference. But when motions and gestures are undertaken for a *reason*, as a symbol of a disposition of heart or as an "acted prayer," they can bring a richness of embodied meaning to the shared liturgical action.

Be Mindful

Maintain an inner awareness of your own movements of the spirit, thoughts, feelings, prayers, aspirations, joys during the conduct of the service. How does the liturgy move you in ways that you would not be moved in ordinary experience? How does the inner process of your own worship reveal or illuminate or influence your participation in elements of the liturgy? On more than one occasion I have begun a worship service feeling tired or distracted or irritable, and have discovered that the progress of the liturgy, the rhythm of the songs and prayers, the voices of other people in dialogue and response, even the shape of the space and the presence of other bodies in the room, have all contributed to constitute a spiritual environment in which my own mood has been uplifted and transformed and made more open to the creative call of God. The inner and the outer, the personal and the communal, the private and the public are woven together in ritual action; and being mindful of that weaving is one of the primary exercises that can make liturgy a truly spiritual practice.

A process spirituality can bring a special emphasis to the role of the body and the importance of the community in any spiritual discipline. These factors are also key elements in ritual, ceremony, and liturgy. For a process spirituality, then, active participation in lively and creative liturgy can be a significant spiritual practice.

A process spirituality can bring a special emphasis to the role of the body and the importance of the community in any spiritual discipline. These factors are also key elements in ritual, ceremony, and liturgy. For a process spirituality, then, active participation in lively and creative liturgy can be a significant spiritual practice.

Notes

1. *Adventures of Ideas* (New York: The Free Press, 1967), 265.
2. Contemporary commentators often translate the Greek word *leitourgia*, from which we derive the word liturgy, as "the work of the people." Strictly speaking, that is a mistranslation; while the two root words do mean "people's work," in ancient secular Greek the word was used to mean "a public work undertaken at private expense," such as when a private benefactor paid for the repair of a road or the sponsorship of a theatrical performance. Christians adopted the word for their prayer services in the belief that their ceremonies were for the common good of the whole world, and therefore were *their* public work undertaken at private expense. Still, mistranslation or no, the phrase "work of the people" conveys an important truth about the nature of liturgy.

PART TWO

4

Spirituality and Sensory Perception
John B. Cobb, Jr.

5

An Advenurous Spirituality
Bruce G. Epperly

6

A Spirituality of Discernment
Paul S. Nancarrow

FOUR

Spirituality and Sensory Perception

John B. Cobb, Jr.

So what is spirituality in general? One form, I think, is mind-altering. That is, some spiritual disciplines lead, or can lead, to perceiving what is not ordinarily experienced. Drugs have been used as a shortcut to such extraordinary experience, but many realize that this shortcut has limitations and should be avoided. Of course, such experiences can also occur unsought. They are certainly a matter of great interest, but I will not discuss them further.

The other form of spirituality is a heightening of elements that are present in ordinary experience. This heightening is what goes on to some extent in the typical service of worship. We become more aware of our dependence on God, of God's generosity to us, and of the possibilities of new life. For most of us, most of the time, these possibilities do not constitute a wholly new sensibility, but worship serves to keep them important. When these elements, which are usually vague in our pervasive experience, are not lifted up and emphasized, they are likely to fade into ineffectiveness.

Aspects of our experience may be valued negatively as they are brought to focused attention. Often in worship we are reminded that we do not respond to God's generosity as we should. Some Christians examine their motives in order to detect the selfish elements in them. In some forms of spirituality people lift up their sexual appetites in order to intensify feelings of guilt and shame.

Every practice of this type of spirituality thus reflects the valuation of aspects of our experience as desirable or undesirable. As our values change, so does our spirituality. Today most of us appraise the natural world, including our bodies, positively, and want to heighten awareness of these. Traditionally, Christians sought to transcend the natural, if not to vilify it.

As I noted in Chapter One, in developing my own understanding of Christianity in general and spirituality in particular, I have found the Whiteheadian model of human experience particularly useful. I believe it supports the values of many contemporary Christians. For me, it clarifies the elements in experience that contemporary Christians most prize and also makes clearer how they can be accentuated and developed. With that in mind, let us examine the Whiteheadian model more closely.

Whitehead took experience as the basic reality. In this he resembled the philosophical idealists. But he understood that *human* experience is just one of many types of experience. Whatever exists is something for itself as well as something for others. Accordingly, everything is an act of experience, whether conscious or unconscious. He calls all creaturely things "actual occasions."

The foregoing formulation may be misleading. Most of the things we think about are not strictly actual occasions. They are made up of many actual occasions. A plant is not an actual occasion. It is made up of cellular and molecular occasions. Each of these is momentary; so we may think of a plant as a vast complex society of such momentary occurrences. It is these individual occurrences that are something in and for themselves, as well as something for all those other actual occasions that follow them. The sorts of things we usually talk about are all societies. Most of them have no subjectivity except in their individual members.

The case of animals is somewhat different. They too, are societies of cells and molecules. But in vertebrate animals, the central nervous system gives rise in the region of the brain to an especially complex actual occasion, one which is characterized in part by consciousness. Whitehead calls this the presiding occasion. Its subjectivity is far richer than that of the many occasions in the body that contribute to it. Also, its decisions have far more effect on the other occasions that make up the psychophysical organism than any one of those other occasions. On the other hand, collectively those other occasions extensively determine the experience of the presiding occasion. The relation is one of interdependence and interconnection.

The actual occasions of greatest interest to us are those in which our own consciousness occurs. These are presiding occasions that arise in our own bodies. Whitehead calls a succession of these occasions, such as the flow of experience with which I identify myself, a "soul." There are dog souls, and whale souls, as well as human souls. If the term "soul" is too laden with religious connotations, we can use the Greek word it translates: "psyche." An animal—including the human animal—is a unity of soul and body or a psychosomatic whole.

But in Whitehead's analysis, this is a very complex unity with blurred boundaries. Within it we can make many distinctions. The distinction between soul and body, or psyche and soma, is one of these. They are interconnected and interdependent, but they are also distinct. In addition, the body has many members that play diverse roles in relation to one another. Some even continue to live for a long time after the body as a whole has died. Some are easily affected by the presiding occasion whereas others are not.

One main role of the body is to connect the psyche to the environment especially through the organs of sense. The data of these organs tend to dominate consciousness, so that we are more aware of the feel and color of the environment than of the events in our bodies that mediate these data. For example, we are sometimes aware of the feelings of our eyes, but unless they are irritated in some way, this feeling is much less intense than that of the colored world the eyes make real for us. It is striking how often philosophers talk about the colored objects in this world given to us through the eyes without mentioning the role of the human body. The essential role of the nerves leading from the eyes to the brain and of the occipital lobe are even more neglected since in general we have no consciousness of these at all.

In his analysis of perception, Whitehead engages in what today we would call "deconstruction." What we ordinarily think of as perception, e.g., seeing the white ball, is analyzed into two perceptive modes. First, the events in the region of the white ball reflect light that stimulates the cells in the eye and sends messages to the brain. This is perception in the mode of causal efficacy. Although light travels very fast indeed, and nerve impulses are transmitted through the body at astonishing speeds, there is some lapse of time between the events in the region of the ball and their effect on our brain. This becomes important when we are engaged in astronomical observations.

Second, the brain projects on the environment a patch of color. Normally this appears to us at virtually the same location where the ball is. But when we look at the night sky, the place that we see a planet is not where the planet now is but where it was when the light now affecting us left it. This patch of color is presented to us as there now. Whitehead calls it perception in the mode of presentational immediacy. In the language common to our time, our brain constructs the world that is most vividly presented to us, the world of *sensa*. However, it does not construct it out of nothing. It constructs it, normally, out of the causal effects of the environment upon it.

Our normal sense experience is the integration of these two modes. Hence, we perceive real things, such as the ball, as having particular characteristics, in this case, whiteness. This has led us to think of a world of substances with attributes, a self-existing object, the ball, with the attribute of whiteness. Critical philosophical analysis has deconstructed that way of thinking for philosophers, although it continues to pervade common sense.

The result in the history of Western philosophy has been to abandon realism. We suppose that we cannot get behind the appearances or phenomena given us in what Whitehead understands to be perception in the mode of presentational immediacy to anything that is really there outside of ourselves. The strong tendency in recent thought is toward solipsism. Since Immanuel Kant, the emphasis has been on how the world in which we live is constructed by us. For Kant there was little freedom in how we constructed it, but beginning with Hegel, there has been emphasis on the diverse ways in which it is constructed in different cultures and cultural epochs and by different individuals in the same epoch.

From a Whiteheadian point of view, there is much of value in this tradition. We do construct the worlds of which we are most clearly conscious. But it is equally important to recognize that we do not construct the world as such. In every moment a world is given to us. We are what we are and construct as we do largely because of the causal efficacy of that world. That world is what it is, whatever constructive work we do upon it. To emphasize only our constructive work, and not the givenness and efficacy of nature and of other people, is profoundly dangerous.

We are saying, on the one hand, that something is given and that this is not the patches of color that are visually projected. We are saying, on the other hand, that what are given are not substances in the usual sense of that term. What then can the given reality be?

To get a clue as to what is given and efficacious in our experience, we can examine an aspect of that experience that has not played a prominent role in Western philosophy, namely, the way one moment of that experience is real for, and efficacious in, its successor. Consider your own experience in this respect. My experience is that what I become in one moment is very largely a continuation and development out of what I became in the preceding moment. That preceding moment lives on in the present one. It is past, but being past does not mean that it no longer participates in the present.

One way of focusing this is to think of your experience as you listen to music. In one moment you may be hearing the final chord of a musical phrase. But to hear it as the completion of a musical phrase requires that the antecedent moments, in which you heard the earlier chords in that phrase, still resonate in the present. Your present experience must include much of these earlier experiences. It includes them as past, but as a past that is alive in the present.

Whitehead calls this relation between the present and the immediate past a "prehension." If you understand what a prehension is, you will understand Whitehead's most important contribution to human thought generally, and to reflection on spirituality in particular. You will be able to talk realistically about many of the things the Bible talks about and that religious people have affirmed over the ages. The narrow limitations modernity has imposed on religious discourse, and on scientific discourse as well, disappear.

I need to unpack this a bit. According to the dominant philosophical traditions, our knowledge of the world, indeed, of everything other than our immediate experience, is mediated to us through sense experience. This sense experience is limited to Whitehead's perception in the mode of presentational immediacy. On this view, any knowledge that is not given in that mode has to be derived by reasoning from the data it provides.

Given these assumptions, it is quite obvious that there can be no immediate experience of God. If we are to believe in God at all, it is either based on a rational deduction from sense experience or is a blind leap of faith. The alternative is that it is supernaturally implanted. Of course, we may argue that there is some other access to the divine, such as intuition. But in the modern context, claims to intuition fare badly.

Once we understand the primacy of prehensions, the situation is drastically changed. Note that in the primary example I gave you, the datum of the prehension is a subject. The present moment of experience is receiving into itself the antecedent moments of experience. Also, sense experience plays no role in this relation as such. I do not see or hear or smell or touch the antecedent moments of my experience.

Of course, in my example, part of what is prehended is the enjoyment of certain sounds in the antecedent occasion. But the present prehension of that past enjoyment is not sensory. We could discuss the transmission of emotions from occasion to occasion without any reference to the world of sense experience at all. Perception in the mode of presentational immediacy, far from being primary, is derivative from perception in the mode of causal efficacy. This latter is constituted in very complex ways by the sort of prehension of which I gave the relation to one's own immediate past as an example.

The primary element in all experience is nonsensory. It relates us to other subjects rather than to the world of objects that we ordinarily project on our environment. Accordingly, the idea that we also experience God is not problematic as it is when sense experience is considered primary. If there is a God, a Whiteheadian would expect that we prehend God and that God, in turn, prehends us. In fact, Whitehead develops a quite elaborate doctrine of the role that God plays in creaturely experience. His philosophical theories are congenial to many biblical themes.

It is not only in relation to God that the idea of prehension opens up possibilities that the modern Western tradition has obscured. We do not prehend only the past occasions that make up our personal lives. We also prehend the neuronal occasions in the brain and, through them, other cellular occasions in our bodies. These prehensions are also of subjects. In other words, our bodies are not mere objects to be manipulated but societies of subjects with which we have close kinship.

Our relations to the environment of our bodies are also prehensions. That means that what we prehend are actual occasions each of which is a subject, that is, something in and for itself. These actual occasions are realizations of value. The world is not simply an objective machine but a living, feeling context for our lives and feelings. Our feelings derive in large part from the feelings of our bodies and of their environments.

Of course, this is especially important with respect to other people. We do not have to infer from sensory experience that other people are subjects like ourselves. We prehend them as such. Their subjectivity affects ours. This may be particularly true of an infant's relation to its mother, but it applies broadly to social relationships. It is depressing to be with depressed people, and it is usually exhilarating to be in an excited and enthusiastic group.

I am deriving little from this Whiteheadian model that I could not derive directly from the Bible. The materialistic view of nature and the modern epistemological views, which make normal Christian spirituality so problematic today, obviously do not affect the scriptures. But they have affected the interpretation of the Bible so much, and for so long, that something is needed to free us to recover the sense of immediacy in relation to God and to the natural world that the biblical authors generally took for granted.

In this respect, it is helpful to recall the theology of John Wesley and the distinctiveness of his contribution. At the heart of Wesley's theology was his understanding of God's grace. Certainly grace was central also for Luther and Calvin. We are justified by grace through faith. Nothing is theologically more important than that. But for Luther and Calvin, at least in their primary emphasis, this grace does not operate directly in the believer's experience. It occurs in the mind of God. God graciously forgives us. When we believe that God has done this, then we are freed from the burden of trying to justify ourselves. This is a real change. When we do not experience the need to justify ourselves, we can be open to the neighbor as the other rather than being preoccupied with ourselves. In no way did Wesley minimize the truth and importance of this conviction that God loves and forgives us regardless of our sinfulness. Nor do I.

But Wesley believed that something else happens. God's grace or Spirit works directly in us transformatively. It is this transforming presence of God within us that brings us to justifying grace. It continues to work transformatively within us in strengthening our love of God and neighbor and thus sanctifying us.

This is the clear difference between Wesley and the earlier

Reformers. For the earlier Reformers, the relation of God and human beings is essentially external. God is gracious, and when people realize that, their life orientation is changed. The Reformers believed that the rise of faith in the believer was also an act of divine grace. Hence they also believed that God acts within the believer. But the general impression given by their formulations is that even the act of God that introduces something new in the believer comes from without. Its occurrence is supernatural, that is, it is an intervention of God into the ordinary course of events.

Wesley was not satisfied with this externalistic view of the relation of God and the world. He believed that God was in the world, especially in human beings. Human beings are what they are, in part, because of the working of God within them. This universal internal working of the Spirit moves people toward faith. Of course, God is outside of people as well. God pervades the universe. God's love for human beings is characteristic of God's own interior and independent life. Nothing creatures do can change the character of God. But the God whose love for us is so important expresses that love, not only in forgiveness of sins, but also in actively and directly transforming us.

In my opinion Wesley was more faithful to Paul than were the earlier Reformers. Paul speaks of Christ and of the Spirit as being in us. One verse that Wesley particularly loved to quote says that God's Spirit witnesses with our spirits that we are children of God (Romans 8:16). It would be easy to say that the difference between Wesley and the earlier Reformers was that they emphasized God's transcendence where Wesley gave equal emphasis to God's immanence. This is correct as far as it goes. But the spirituality to which a doctrine of divine immanence gives rise differs according to just how that immanence is understood and the role that the immanent God is understood to play within us.

In Wesley's day, the church was very much opposed to what was called "enthusiasm," and Wesley was repeatedly accused of this. Today, United Methodists wish we were guilty of what we call "enthusiasm," but this is not the same. In Wesley's day the word meant possession by divinity. In the twentieth century, the phenomenon the eighteenth-century church feared returned in the form of Pentecostalism and the charismatic movement. My interest here is not to reject those developments or to deny that experience of this type occurs. Also, in these large movements there are varieties of doctrines and forms of spirituality. Still, I do want to indicate that the immanence they emphasize differs from that described by Wesley. Accordingly, a Wesleyan spirituality differs from a charismatic one.

The basic model of the enthusiasts is more like that of the Reformers than that of Wesley. That is, God is thought of as normally external to human beings. The difference with the Reformers is that whereas the latter saw God's intervention in human life in very limited ways, such as the gift of faith, the enthusiasts believed that God could take over control of the whole of human experience, at least intermittently. The human center of human experience and life could be replaced by the incursion of God. What is said and done in this condition is understood to be the unilateral action of God through the human body.

In the ancient world the sibyls were understood to prophesy in this way. In the early church, the Montanist prophetess belonged to this tradition. The Fundamentalist view of the inspiration of the Bible and the Muslim view of the writing of the Qur'an belong to this family of ideas. In the twentieth century, speaking in tongues can be interpreted along these lines. This may be a valid form of experience, but it is not the type of spirituality congruent with Wesley's understanding. For him the Spirit is always present within the person and drawing the person toward fuller life. The Spirit does not enter an already complete person from without and displace the human self. The Spirit always participates in the constitution of the person.

In a very loose sense, Wesley's understanding can be called mystical. And at times he was strongly drawn toward mystical writings. He adapted many of these writings for the devotional life of his followers. On the other hand, he felt that the Christian mystics understated the importance of what the Reformers had emphasized, our dependence on God's act of forgiving us in connection with the work of Christ. He also opposed any idea of losing one's individual selfhood in union with God. He thought that the talk of the dark night of the soul reflected too great an emphasis on human effort to rise to God and too little attention to the actual transformation effected by the Holy Spirit.

A Whiteheadian spirituality will center on the transforming work of the Spirit working in us. That work, Wesley makes clear, is primarily to be understood as the increase of our love for God and for God's creatures. Of course, other people are the most important creatures we are to love, but, quite surprisingly for an eighteenth-century thinker, Wesley was concerned for the well-being of animals as well. To grow spiritually is to love God's creatures—especially, but not exclusively—the human ones, more.

Within the Christian life, Wesley thought that all actions were governed by love. But he understood that for many Christians this required effort. Even among sincere believers, there are strong impulses to put oneself first, to be indifferent to the needs of others, even to treat them as threats or enemies. The Christian avoids acting on these self-centered tendencies, but this life of struggle to control that within oneself which is less than love is not the ideal Christian life.

As we grow in grace in that process that Wesley called sanctification, love comes to play a larger role in our actual motives. We do not have to work so hard to control other motives, because they grow weaker. We act for the sake of others because we really want their good. The ultimate goal of spiritual growth is for love to be so dominant in our actual feelings toward others that no effort is required to act only from love. The ideal is a stage in life when we express love to all our neighbors spontaneously.

Wesley knew that social reinforcement is important to spiritual growth. Hence he organized new believers in groups where they took responsibility for one another and shared their problems, their successes, and their failures. There is much wisdom in that, and Wesley would not approve the extreme privacy and individualism of much of what is called spirituality today. His spirituality cultivates love, whether it is cultivated in solitude or in groups.

Having followed Wesley to this point, I acknowledge that I think there were limitations in his way of understanding human beings and God that restrict the adequacy of his teaching for us. Accordingly, I turn also to Whitehead for help.

First, Wesley's understanding of love focused on what is called *agape* in the New Testament. This is immensely important. But the New Testament also speaks of compassion, and this is equally important. We want other people to help us in our need, but we also want to be understood and accepted for what we are. Whitehead's model provides a more balanced account of these two forms of loving relationship. They are both grounded in the fundamental metaphysical situation. We come into being in each moment by conforming to the past in many respects. That is, we feel anew what was felt in the past. We constitute ourselves out of that past with reference to the future. We have some concern about that future. But it is often far too narrow.

Second, Wesley separated our love of God and our love of neighbor too sharply. He recognized some problems with his own account of how we are to love God. He taught, as Whitehead later did, that God is in us and that we are in God, but when he talked of love of God, these aspects of his thought did not come to the fore. I believe that we can understand the meaning of loving God better through following Whitehead's account.

Third, Wesley did not reflect much on our relation to our bodies. In general, over the centuries, Christians have thought of the body as something to be disciplined and controlled. In the tradition, it has been especially associated with sexual temptation. This plays a remarkably small role in Wesley's reflection. But the celebration of the body and the openness to learning from the wisdom of the body are twentieth-century developments that Wesley did not anticipate. If we want to cultivate a love of our bodies, Whitehead proves more helpful.

In relation to the natural environment generally, Wesley places no obstacles in the way of our cultivation of a loving relationship. But he offers little help. He was appalled by the suffering we inflict on other animals, and this is a remarkable sensitivity for Christians of his time. But a sense of kinship with these creatures, and a deep appreciation of our connectedness to the whole web of life and its inorganic base, are sensitivities that have come into our churches only in recent decades. Whitehead can help us to articulate and develop these in ways that go beyond Wesley.

In a Christian spirituality, love of the "neighbor" is understood to include all creatures. There is nothing esoteric about this. It belongs to the heart of ordinary Christian piety. But I believe that a Whiteheadian understanding of the Christian life can undergird and make such a spirituality effective.

FIVE

An Adventurous Spirituality

Bruce G. Epperly

Process theology affirms a spirituality of adventure. Faithfulness to God calls us to become God's partners in the evolving adventure of creative transformation of ourselves, our communities, and the planet. While many spiritual teachers describe God in terms of changeless perfection, process theology describes divine perfection in terms of dynamic and intimate, creative and responsive love. God is constantly providing an ever-changing world with novel visions and possibilities and the energy and inspiration to seek their embodiment in the concrete realities of everyday life. Accordingly, the goal of spiritual formation is to experience and respond to God's life-transforming presence and in the here and now rather than to abstract and disembodied spiritual truths.

Process theology affirms the insights of the Christian theological and spiritual tradition as essential to our spiritual identities. But, it equally recognizes that spiritual growth embraces the wisdom of the past in the context of commitment to the future toward which God leads the universe moment by moment. Contrary to certain forms of religion, process theology recognizes that the Divine Eros is the ultimate source of spiritual restlessness and adventure. God is always doing a new thing and calls us to do likewise!

The adventures of a day, a lifetime, or a planet have no predetermined destination, but are lived out in the context of an open-ended, lively, and God-inspired universe. Our daily pilgrimage resembles the adventures of ancient pilgrims whose journeys took them to unknown lands without the benefit of map or compass. Lured forward by the Divine Eros, their days were filled with surprise and wonder, and challenge and threat. They faced mysterious frontiers, knowing that God was their most intimate companion and guide.

It has been said that "God is the circle, whose center is everywhere, and whose circumference is nowhere." This aphorism points to the lively dance of divine omnipresence, omniscience, and omni-activity. Our adventures take place in a divine environment in which the concrete realities of God's inspiration, companionship, and knowledge shape one another and condition our spiritual lives, albeit primarily unconsciously. With the apostle Paul, process theologians affirm that within the liveliness of God's presence "we live, move, and have our being" (Acts 17:28) and that through God's presence in Christ, God seeks to "reconcile to [Godself] all things" (Colossians 1:20). In the spirit of the Psalmist, process thought affirms that wherever our adventures lead us, we are always accompanied by an Adventurer who provides protection as well as challenge.

> Where can I go from your spirit?
> Or where can I flee from your presence?
> If I ascend to heaven, you are there;

If I make my bed in Sheol, you are there.
If I take the wings of the morning
and settle at the farthest ends of the sea,
even there your hand shall lead me,
and your right hand shall hold me fast. (Psalm 139:7–10)

Spiritual adventure is grounded in—and inspired by—a holy imagination in which we experience deeper dimensions of reality and ourselves than meet the eye. With biblical scholar Walter Brueggemann, process theologians see the task of spiritual leaders, prophets, and ordinary persons as exploring alternative visions of reality to that of the present situation. From this perspective, there are no ordinary persons or times, but rather extraordinary opportunities to experience the divine adventure in every day life. In the spirit of Celtic spirituality, process theology sees all places as "thin places," revealing God's protean vision for persons and the planet.

When my son Matthew was a young child, we often read books from a series entitled, "Choose Your Own Adventure." In these books, a child was invited to decide which path he or she would take when confronted by alternative possibilities. One choice might lead to buried treasure, the other to a dungeon or an encounter with a prince, princess, or dragon. Yet, each choice, despite its positive or negative outcome, led to other choices along the adventure of the character's and the child's journey. Process theology reminds us that all of life is an adventure in which we are invited to "choose our own adventure" in companionship with God's Holy Adventure. Accordingly, process spirituality awakens our imaginations as a means of discerning God's adventurous presence in our daily lives. In the following sections, we explore a spiritual pathway that joins both novelty and security in our spiritual adventures. We will discover that process spirituality provides a lively interpretation of traditional spiritual practices. With John Wesley, process theology calls us to a life of spiritual growth and social holiness.

Finding Your Spiritual Center

The divine center is everywhere. Wherever our adventures of ideas or geography take us, God is our adventurous companion. One of the great insights of the Hebraic tradition was the discovery that the Holy One was not bound by politics, geography, or ethnicity. When Abraham and Sarah wander from the security of their homeland to the mysterious land of divine promise, they initially erect altars at every stopping point. I suspect that, at first, they sought to summon God to their worship centers. Eventually, they erected altars to remind themselves that the One who inspired them to leave their familiar land would always be their constant companion on a surprising adventure.

Centuries later, Celtic spiritual guides also embarked on challenging journeys in which they were threatened by stormy seas and angry foes. Some even set sail on choppy seas with neither compass nor rudder, trusting that God would guide their skiff on a holy adventure. It was customary when they set out on a journey to say a prayer and draw a circle around themselves as a sign of divine omnipresence and protection.

Today, process spirituality embraces the wisdom of the "caim," or prayer of encircling. While process theologians recognize that life is filled with risks and that faith cannot protect us from every threat, they also recognize that God is present as a force for wholeness and reconciliation in every situation. The prayer of encircling is a reminder of God's encircling love and care during our daily pilgrimage. The omni-active and omnipresent God addresses us in every encounter and provides a way when there is no way at every impasse. This prayer may be done as a body prayer or, if you are unable to draw a circle around yourself, you may imagine yourself within the divine circle of inspiration and care.

As you stand, imagine yourself at the center of a divine circle. As you extend your arm, point your index finger outward. Then slowly rotate toward the right in a circular fashion. As you gently rotate, you may say a prayer for protection or inspiration, such as one of the following:

> God protect me on this journey.
> Surround me, whether I walk, drive, or fly.
> Fill my heart and mind with surprising possibilities.
> Remind me that I am always in the circle of your love.
> Remind me this day, O Holy Adventure,
> that your inspiration guides me in every situation.
> Open my eyes to your presence in each meal,
> As I turn on my computer, As I start my car.
> Awaken me to possibility and wonder.
> Energize me to love and embrace all I meet.

As a child, friend, or spouse begins his or her daily adventure, you may circle them in your imagination with a prayer such as the following:

> Keep_____ in the circle of your love.
> In every situation, remind them of your presence
> and awaken them to possibility and wonder.
> Let them live by your love.

A well-known Celtic prayer, attributed to St. Patrick, captures the essence of companionship with the Holy Adventure. Our prayers do not invoke a distant and apathetic God, but awaken us to God's presence and to new possibilities as a result of our holy awareness. Our consciousness of divine companionship enables God to be present in our lives with greater energy and possibility.

> Christ behind and before me,
> Christ beneath and above me,
> Christ around and about me,
> Christ on my left and on my right,
> Christ when I rise in the morning,
> Christ when I lie down at night.

Holy Imagination

Process theology affirms the ubiquity of divine revelation. The heavens declare the glory of God, but so do the cells of our body and the embraces of lovers. As Meister Eckhardt proclaims, "all things are words of God." Accordingly, in contrast to certain conservative Christians, process theology affirms that the Bible is but *one* revelation of God. Further, the revelatory power of scripture did not end with the closing of the canon, but occurs whenever the scriptures are read, pondered, or preached. Building on the Wesleyan quadrilateral, process theologians see divine revelation as the dynamic and evolving interplay of scripture, reason, experience, and tradition along with the insights of science, literature, culture, and the arts. Indeed, your own spiritual experiences are part of God's ongoing and evolving revelation to humankind. Imagination is an essential aspect of the spiritual journey and the encounter with scripture. A holy imagination enables us to become contemporaries with the ancient words of scripture as our own interpretations shed new light on their meaning. While divine revelation is universal, it is also always intimate and personal in nature.

Jesus of Nazareth invited persons to image God's presence through his use of parables. The New Testament parables not only presented the listener with a reversal of expectations and new ways of looking at God's presence in the world, but also invited the hearer, in the spirit of Wisdom literature, to experience divine revelation in the ordinary and often overlooked moments of life. Fifteen centuries later, Ignatius of Loyola, the founder of the Jesuits, invited persons to read scripture with all their senses while placing themselves within the biblical narrative itself.[1] We are invited in the *Spiritual Exercises of Ignatius of Loyola* to experience the environmental setting of a biblical event, to envisage the characters involved, and to see ourselves as persons called by God through the events described by scripture. Whether we refer to this practice as guided imagination, imaginative prayer, or holy imagination, the use of the imagination enables us to become artists and co-creators in the evolving understanding of scripture. God is still speaking, and each moment reveals divine wisdom and guidance.

While there are many approaches to imaginative prayer, here is an approach that I have found helpful as a retreat leader and spiritual guide.[2]

Begin the practice of imaginative prayer with a time of silent centering, first by relaxing your body and mind, beginning with the top of the head and working downward to the soles of the feet as you breathe deeply and slowly. Then, meditatively read the scripture passage, in this case, the story of Jesus calming a storm at sea. (Luke 8:22–25) After a few moments of silence, begin the meditation with the reminder that this is a creative adventure and that the participant may shape it as her or his spirit desires.

> *Imagine a beautiful, sunny day. You and a group of friends are going sailing with Jesus. As you prepare to set sail, imagine the scene ... the lake ... the sky ... the horizon.*
>
> *Who is going with you? What do they look like?*

You and your friends have had a successful journey and are planning to celebrate. What foods will you bring with you? What drink? Take time to enjoy the prospect of a lovely sail across the lake.

As you set forth, experience your sail boat skimming gently across the lake. Feel the gentle wind, the warm sun.

Suddenly, without warning everything changes. The sky grows dark, the wind begins whip your boat, lighteing flashes, and thunder blasts. Visualize the storm growing stronger and more threatening until your sail boat is engulfed by the storm. Experience your boat being battered by wind, wave, and rain as if it were a toy. How do you feel? How do your companions respond to the storm?

As you experience the storm at sea, reflect a moment on your own life in which you are currently struggling for "survival": what are the storms in your life today? How do they batter and buffet your life? What resources do you have as you face the storms of life?

As the storms batter your craft, you cry out to God. Then, you remember that Jesus is with you in the boat, quietly present in the midst of the storm. How do you feel when you remember that Jesus is with you? How does this change your attitude toward the storm?

Jesus comes to the deck and gently speaks, "Peace. Be still" to the storm. The storm quiets gradually until once more the day is clear and sunny. You and your companions sail gently to the harbor across the lake. Take a moment to claim your positive emotions. Take a moment to express your gratitude for God's presence in the storms of life as you arrive on shore safe and ready for the next adventure.

You may choose to journal your experience as a way of further encountering God's presence in the text of your life.

Holy Reading

Process theology affirms that our understanding of scripture is contextual and personal in nature. Further, as a living word, the meaning of scripture is constantly being transformed as we relate it to the challenges of our own lives. Still, often we are trapped by traditional, outmoded, and dysfunctional understandings of scripture that prevent us from experiencing God's living presence within the scriptural words. This is especially true of passages that have often been used to perpetuate biblical literalism, sexism, exclusivism, or homophobia. We may even abandon scripture altogether as a result of our inability to experience scripture in new and unexpected ways.

In many ways, process theology affirms the insights of our Jewish spiritual parents who saw scripture as a living, changing document. According to the rabbinical tradition, fidelity to divine revelation was to be found in our willingness to question scripture itself, challenge earlier—and even "orthodox"—interpretations of scripture, and boldly articulate insightful interpretations of our own. We can see this process of transforming the text in new ways in Job's challenge of traditional understandings of the sources of suffering and Jesus' dynamic affirmation and reinterpretation of scripture in the Sermon on the Mount and sabbath encounters. Process spiritual formation, in this spirit, revives the wisdom of the *midrash*, the belief that the spirit constantly inspires our reading and hearing of scripture in novel and meaningful ways.

The path of holy reading, or *lectio divina*, initially taught by Benedict of Narsia, provides one way to hear the scripture in a new and lively way.[3] Along with imaginative prayer, *lectio divina* reminds us that the white spaces in scripture are just as important as the written words in terms of understanding God's presence in our lives. Apart from an imaginative encounter that enables us to experience scripture in new and surprising ways, scripture may become a dead and spiritually oppressive text.

Updated for the twenty-first century, *lectio divina* or holy reading, can be practiced according to the following pattern:

1. A time of quiet relaxation and centering, grounded in a willingness to hear God's intimate and personal word.
2. A prayer for insight and awareness of God's aim for our lives in the reading of scripture.
3. Reading or listening to the scripture two or three times slowly and quietly.
4. A time of quiet reflection on what has been heard or read.
5. Awareness of a particular word or phrase or image that bursts forth from scripture. Quiet reflection and repetition of the word, image, or phrase.
6. Meditation on the meaning of the word for your life.
7. Meditation on what changes might occur in your life if you were to take the word seriously.
8. Silent reflection on the meaning of your prayerful experience.
9. Closing prayer of thanksgiving and commitment to following your new insights in daily life.

In the spirit of the Benedictine tradition, holy reading may be practiced in the form of a sitting meditation or a walking prayer.

Affirmative Awareness

While divine revelation is universal, our ability to experience God's presence in our lives is shaped by focusing on certain affirmations of faith. Like searchlights, these affirmations not only shape our experience of the world, but also transform our minds. The use of affirmations reminds us that healing involves the transformation of the mind as well as our bodies and spirits. Process theology affirms the Pauline insight, "be not conformed to the world, but be transformed by the renewing of your mind" (Romans 12:2).

Spiritual formation relates to both the conscious and unconscious mind. Psychologists and spiritual guides remind us that our unconscious attitudes, grounded in early childhood experiences and cultural archetypes, shape our interpretations of the events of our lives. Accordingly, unconscious images of self-worth, embodiment, relationships, can either limit or liberate us. While affirmations begin initially with the conscious repetition of statements of fact, they eventually begin to transform and heal the unconscious mind as well. Although spiritual affirmations may, at first, seem counterfactual, they describe our deepest identity and reality as God's beloved children. The use of spiritual affirmations is a reminder that God's aim is wholeness for the unconscious as well as conscious mind and that is just as active in the "sighs too deep for words" as our theological doctrines.

The following affirmations arise out from the insights of process theology and spiritual formation.

> *God is constantly inspiring me with new possibilities. Each moment reveals God's presence in my life.*
>
> *I open myself to God's surprising possibilities in my life. God guides me each moment of the day.*
>
> *God is present in all things. My life matters to God.*
>
> *I am open to creative transformation in every life experience.*

With God as my companion, every moment is a holy moment.

There are no "dead ends." Even in difficult situations, God presents me with possibilities for growth and healing.

The following lively affirmations arise out of a dynamic, life-supporting encounter with the biblical tradition.

God is transforming my mind. (Romans 12:2)

God is always with me. (Psalm 139)

I am always in God's presence. (Psalm 46:10)

I am the light of the world. (Matthew 5:13–16)

God supplies my deepest needs. (Philippians 4:19–20)

My faith is making me whole. (Mark 5:34)

God's light shines in me. (John 1:9)

I am God's beloved daughter (or son). (Luke 3:22)

My body is the temple of God. (I Corinthians 6:19–20)

Process spirituality enables us to become God's lively and insightful companions as we enter the biblical narrative. God is always doing a new thing in our lives and revealing new and surprising wisdom as we open to surprising revelations through scripture, spiritual practices, worship, and service.

Notes

1. See David L. Fleming, S.J., *What Is Ignatian Spirituality?* (Chicago: Loyola Press, 2008) and St. Ignatius of Loyola, trans. George Ganss, S.J., *The Spiritual Exeercises of St. Loyola* (Chicago: Loyola Press, 1992).

2. This exercise is adapted from Bruce Epperly, *The Power of Affirmative Faith* (St. Louis: Chalice, 2001). For other guided prayers inspired by process theology, see *The Power of Affirmative Faith* as well as Bruce Epperly, *God's Touch: Faith, Wholeness, and the Healing Miracles of Jesus* (Philadelphia: Westminster/John Knox, 2001); and Bruce Epperly and Lewis Solomon, *Mending the World* (Philadelphia/ Minneapolis: Innisfree/Augsburg, 2003); *Walking in the Light* (St. Louis: Chalice, 2004); *Finding Angels in Boulders* (St. Louis: Chalice, 2005).

3. See Norvene Vest, *Preferring Christ* and Kathleen Norris, *Cloister Walk*.

SIX

A Spirituality of Discernment

Paul S. Nancarrow

Process theology affirms that God is active in every moment of experience, providing new possibilities for each occasion, giving aims for action and lures for feeling for every actual entity. In moments of human experience, these aims from God are usually below the threshold of consciousness: they play an important role in the origination of our experiences, but by the time the data of experience inherited from the past or derived from the world are factored in, the initial aim from God is usually not available for conscious discrimination. One of the functions of spiritual practice, as John Cobb points out in Chapter Four, is "a heightening of elements that are present in ordinary experience"; that is, the special degree of attentiveness achieved in spiritual practice can bring to consciousness things that are usually vague or obscured. Spirituality can help us become more aware of the particular aims and calls God gives us in ordinary experience.

This means that an important aspect of a process spirituality would be a spirituality of discernment. As Bruce Epperly affirms in Chapter Five, God is constantly calling us to join with God in Holy Adventure in the unfolding of the universe. And Cobb, in turn, raises a key question: "How can we distinguish that within our experience which is God's call from the many competing voices that are derived from the past?" Discerning God's aims for us in the midst of ordinary experience is an indispensable element in a Christian process spirituality.

Of all spiritual practices, discernment is one that is perhaps most easily thought of as practiced with a group. Whereas things like prayer or meditation may strike us first as solitary activities and only secondarily as things to be done in concert with others, discernment by its very nature lends itself to dialogue, conversation, sharing questions and insights with other people and trusting in their wisdom to inform and extend our own. If I think I may be discerning God's call to me in a particular situation, but I am also aware that the "call" may be more from my past or my fears than from God, it is helpful to have a friend or a group to whom I can bring my question, and whose discernment can help corroborate or revise my own.

Furthermore, since process theology places special emphasis on *societies* of occasions and the way groups of experiences come together to form new wholes, a process spirituality can place special emphasis on discernment of God's aims for groups as well as for individuals. God may call me to a particular sort of richness of experience in a given situation; but if I am a member of a group, *my* richness of experience may also contribute to the *group's* richness of experience, and the group's to mine, and that combined richness may be an aspect of God's call to the group as a whole. Discerning what the group is called to do, in addition to helping its members discern what they are individually called to do, is also an element in a process spirituality of discernment. There are several practices that can promote discernment in group settings. A process approach to these practices can help us become more aware of, and more responsive to, God's aims for us in everyday life.

Checking In

One very simple spiritual practice that can be used for discernment of God's guidance in group settings is "the check-in." This can be done with all sorts of groups, whether the group has gathered for study or prayer, business or fellowship. On a very simple level, this practice works as an icebreaker, helping members of the group to feel reconnected and reacquainted with each other since their last meeting. On a deeper level, it may elicit into prominence certain spiritual themes or threads of common experience that are at work among the members of the group, and that will therefore have their conditioning influence on the group meeting.

To begin the check-in, the group leader or facilitator can invite each member of the group to consider how they have been aware of God's presence or guidance in the time since they last met. I like to use the questions "Where have you seen God at work in or around you?" or "How is it with your soul?" Each member of the group may then tell a brief story of an event or experience in which they were particularly moved in a way they attribute to God.

While each member is speaking, other members should listen attentively, without interruption for questions or comments. The purpose of sharing the story is not to convey information or solve a problem, but to allow the speaker to reflect on the felt presence of God in the midst of ordinary experience. Simple questions for clarification or detail may be allowed, but it is best if they are kept to a minimum. Group members may speak in order, e.g., simply going around the table clockwise from the leader; I prefer, however, to let members speak at random, as each is moved. Every member should be given the opportunity to speak; no member is required to speak.

During the stories, the leader or facilitator has several important roles to play. She or he should thank each member for sharing a story. It is also important to keep an eye on the time; check-in stories for most group meetings should usually last no more than a minute and a half to two minutes. The leader or facilitator may also need to call group members back to the purpose of the process; at times the telling of stories can devolve toward anecdotal chit-chat or small talk; then the leader should gently ask "Where did you see God in this?" or "How did you feel the Spirit working?" Sometimes it is enough to repeat the leading questions between speakers.

At times the check-in can reveal common themes or issues in the group. A check-in before a parish vestry meeting in my congregation once showed that several members of the group were dealing with grief—a death in the family, a diagnosis of illness, the loss of a job. Because of the check-in, we were able to pray for those in grief; but more than that, we were able to be more attentive to loss-and-redemption themes in the larger issues of parish life the vestry had to deal with in its work during that meeting. Other check-ins may reveal no such common themes; but they do help group members to be more attuned to each other, and more cognizant of the Spirit at work in ordinary circumstances. Because God gives aims to each one of us, in accordance with God's own ideals and our best possibilities, and because God coordinates those aims toward greater realizations of right relationships and peace, we can trust that the threads of experience in our individual lives are also the stuff out of which our common life in Christ is woven. By checking in with each other to share those threads, we can better discern God's call to adventure in our groups as well.

A simpler variation of the check-in I use before worship is an invitation into sacred space. When the congregation has gathered—when the conversations in the entry way have died down, and the greetings to friends have all been made, and *almost* everyone is in their pews and ready to begin—before the opening hymn of the liturgy I greet the people and invite them to prepare their hearts for prayer. I invite people to let the busyness of the outside world recede from their minds, and to hold in their hearts those particular persons or places or concerns they most wish to bring before God in prayer in this liturgy. After a moment of silent prayer, the service begins with the hymn. This entrance rite lacks the conversation and exchange of the check-in; but it does invite worshipers to focus on the particular places in their lives and their actual worlds where they feel God's presence—or the need for God's presence—and it can help the congregation to be more discerning of God at work in the adventure of worship.

Bible Study

Epperly mentions holy reading as a practice for discerning God's aims for our creative adventures. While this is often done in solitude, it may also be done with a group. In fact, it may be even more common in the Christian tradition to read and study the Bible in a group setting than as a solitary act. Cobb refers in Chapter One to the Protestant tradition of reading the Bible in the family. Alan Jones traces the tradition of studying the Bible in community back even farther:

> There is a wonderful passage in Origen where he quotes a Hebrew scholar as saying that the Holy Scriptures are like a large house with many, many rooms and that outside

each door there is a key . . . but it is the wrong key! And to find the right keys that will open the doors, that's a great and arduous task of struggling and being stretched by Scripture. The rabbis said that every word of the Torah has 600,000 faces. Every word, not each chapter or every verse, but every word has 600,000 faces; that is, layers of meaning or entrances, one for each of the children of Israel who stood at the foot of Mt. Sinai. Each face is turned to only one of them. He alone can see it and decipher it. Each person has his own unique access to revelation. And that means that when I read Scripture I can't read Scripture on my own. I won't know what it means without you. And I suggest that what we can't do alone we can do together.[1]

The significance of a passage of scripture is never a simple one-to-one relationship between text and meaning, as if the passage were an equation and its interpretation the solution. Significance and meaning emerge out of a multilayered process of symbolic reference in which words, memories, personal associations, unconscious echoes, archetypal patterns, deeply felt causal efficacies, and aims and lures from God sift and re-sift each other until the many become one in a determinative feeling of connection between the presented text and one's lived experience. That multilayered process is broadened and deepened considerably when engaged with a group.

One very common and very powerful format for the practice of group Bible study goes by various names in different communities and literatures. I've heard it called "African Bible study," "base-community Bible study," "Gospel-based discipleship," and "*lectio divina* for groups." Different practitioners teach minor variations in the format, but the basic outline is as follows:

1. Read aloud the passage to be studied. Take time reading it; do not rush; let each phrase and sentence be savored for its sound and its meaning. (Some groups like to make sure that each member has a printed copy of the passage, so that all can follow along with the reading; I prefer that listeners put aside their texts and simply encounter the passage as a spoken word. We read and we listen with different parts of our brains, and the words can work on us differently through those different modalities. If group members want to refer to the text for questions or clarity later, they may pick up the texts again when the oral reading is complete.)

2. Keep silence for one or two minutes after the reading while group members consider a word or phrase or image from the reading that catches their interest or piques their curiosity or speaks to them in a particularly powerful way.

3. Members share the word or phrase or image that is speaking to them. Participants should simply state what has attracted them, without further elaboration or discussion. Each member listens attentively while the others are speaking, noting how the one passage can contain many points of contact. In this step, and in steps 6 and 9 below, all members are encouraged to share, and no member is required to share.

4. The passage is read again, by a different member of the group. It is desirable to have a variety of voices read the passage; if a woman read the first time, a man should read the second, or vice versa.

5. Keep silence for two or three minutes while group members reflect on what the passage is saying to them

in the particular concrete circumstances of their life and experience.

6. Members share their reflections. Again, their statements should be brief: "What I hear this saying to me is . . ."

7. The passage is read a third time, by yet another different voice.

8. Keep silence for two or three minutes. Each participant reflects on how she or he could respond to the passage's particular meaning as discerned in step 5. If step 5 constitutes a "call," then how does each intend to answer that call?

9. Members share their reflections. This period of sharing may go on at greater length than the previous two. Group members should listen attentively as each one speaks. Some groups may want to allow discussion at this point; members may help each other "test the spirits" in their interpretations, and help the speaker discern if the call is from God, or if there may be other aspects of interpretation that would also be helpful. Other groups may prefer to let each member share reflections without further comment.

10. Pray for each other, for meanings discerned and aims intended.

There are two major strengths in this kind of group Bible study that are particularly germane to a process-relational spirituality. The first is that it opens up a much wider variety of pathways to meaning than any one reader could encounter on his or her own. In process thought, meaning always arises out of relationship, not from some sort of "deposit" of meaning encoded in a word or thing as a bare monad. The wider the field of relationship, the greater the potential for meaning. When many readers contribute to a group process of meaning-making, they bring to the discussion a richness of points of view, alternative interpretations, and contrasts that can illuminate any given text to a much greater depth than a single reader could. For a given passage, one member of a group may be struck by a historical reference; another member may hear in the passage a message of sociopolitical liberation; a third may discern a deeply personal call to decision and action; each of these readers' experiences will be deepened and enriched by encounter with the others. A reader may hear in another's interpretation an aspect of meaning she or he had never considered before, one that may speak deeply to their own needs or aims; listeners may hear in another's response to the passage a call to action that shapes their own intentions to act. The multiple relationships of the group elicit more vectors of meaning from the passage than could be found in solitary study.

The second strength of this study method is the opportunity it affords for "testing the spirits" and mutual corroboration. While all personal interpretations of scripture have some measure of truth to them, not all interpretations are fully adequate to the needs of a given time or place or person, and not all interpretations live up to the full measure of the aims for justice and peace God has for us. As Cobb notes, our capacity for self-deception is great, and there is always the possibility that we may project our own aims onto scripture as much or more than we receive through scripture God's aims for us. Sharing interpretations in group study, and especially sharing our responses and felt calls to action in step 9 of this format, can help cut through self-deceptions to truer discernment of God's guidance. I was in a group Bible study once where one member was wrestling with a decision to move to another city and begin a new career; in his reflection on the passage, he thought he was discerning God's call to "go for it" and take the risk and trust God's providence, but he wasn't sure if that message was coming from the scripture or from his own ambition; he asked the group to listen to his interpretation and test it against their own perceptions of God's will for him. There followed a lively discussion in which not everyone agreed, but from which there emerged a general consensus that his interpretation was true for him, and his decision to move was a response to a genuine call from God. In groups where there is a high level of trust and a genuine knowledge of each other, this kind of mutual discernment and corroboration—or disconfirmation, in some cases—can be very powerful.

Spiritual Direction for Groups

A spiritual practice that was developed in monasteries and convents and has recently emerged into the Protestant mainstream as well, is the practice of spiritual direction. At its simplest, spiritual direction consists of talking with a trusted friend—a "soul friend," Kenneth Leech calls it—who will listen as you speak about your life experience and help you discern therein the movements of God's Spirit. These days, spiritual direction typically takes place in a one-on-one relationship, and spiritual directors typically receive special training to help them be discerning without projecting their own issues onto their directees. But a simple form of spiritual direction can also be practiced in small groups, without the need for special training or leadership. John Ackerman, a Presbyterian pastor and spiritual director, provides some helpful exercises for spiritual direction in groups.[2]

One group practice resembles the check-in, but goes into more detail and depth. It is a version of the "examination of conscience" or *examen* from the Spiritual Exercises of Ignatius of Loyola, adapted for group use. Ackerman calls it the "daily inventory," and uses it in groups with the following script:

- *Close your eyes, please, and focus on your breathing. Let your body be relaxed. "The Lord is my shepherd, I shall not want. He maketh me to lie down in green pastures." Can you let Jesus lead you, to give you what he wants to give in this exercise? Pray for eyes to see, ears to hear.*

- *Go back over the last 24 hours. Is there something that comes to your attention? What is it? [long pause] Go back into the event just for a moment. What might it be saying? Is your response that of gratitude, or is a different prayer called for? What is your prayer? [Pause so that participants can pray.] Now, can you just be with God for a minute, perhaps in the green pasture, beside the still waters. [Again, pause.]*

- *Now take a moment to write down what you noticed.*

- *Then share with a partner, if you care to. Here is some advice: Try to avoid giving advice to the people you listen to. Affirm what seems to be of God. Ask questions to lead to more awareness: This "nothing" that you remember—could God be in the ordinary, in the absence?*

Then move into groups. With the group:

- *Where has the Spirit been as we have been sharing?*
- *Where is there a resonance within you as others shared?*
- *Was there a sense of belonging?*

With the group:

- *Let's be still a moment, and ask the Spirit to guide us, teach us.*
- *Let's go back over the meeting. Where were we working with the*

Spirit, listening to God and each other?

- *When did it seem that we were connected?*
- *Were these moments anything like the time you went back in history and remembered God's touch with you individually, or remembered God's gifts and presence with us together?*[3]

Ackerman's script for a group *examen* operates on the presupposition, congenial to process theology, that God is *always* at work in people's lives. In process terms, we would say that, whether they are explicitly aware of it or not, God is always giving people aims for their moments of experience, God is always receiving into Godself what people have done with God's aims, and God is always fashioning new aims that build upon the past to create the richest experience possible in the next moment. The point of the *examen* is to raise up into consciousness a sequence of divine aims and responses that constitute a thread of God's guidance through a passage of daily experience. The *examen* is a tool for discerning God's guidance amidst the welter of momentary feelings. Ackerman's exercise places this discernment in widening circles of reference: at first one writes one's own discernments privately; then they are shared with a single other; then with a small group; then with the whole group gathered. At each stage, the new circle introduces new connections and contrasts, identifying moments of resonance or belonging or movement that indicate God's presence and work with the group in that moment. This kind of group *examen* can help people discern God's guidance not only in their individual lives, but in the shared lives of their communities.

Another practice of group spiritual direction Ackerman describes is for a three-person small group he calls a *triad*. Each triad consists of a speaker, a listener, and an observer. Triads are often used for role-playing in training situations; e.g., where one person plays a salesperson, another a customer, and the third observes the interaction for later critical review. Ackerman adapts the triad, not as a training tool, but as a way to honor both the subjective and the objective dimensions of spiritual guidance. In this practice:

1. *The* speaker *shares where he or she has noticed God. What is noticed may be exterior or interior, an idea, feeling, sensing, or intuition. The speaker also reports on prayer or prayerfullness, where he or she notices God. The speaker may notice how God responds to prayer. In short, the speaker reports on his or her dialogue with the living God, or God's absence.*

2. *The* listener *has three kinds of responses:*

    - Ordinary encouraging noises: *mmm, ooh, aah. This is paying attention lovingly and prayerfully. You know you are on holy ground.*

    - Evocative questions: *not for information, but to encourage the speaker to notice more. "When your heart was moved, what was that like?" "What is happening now as you recall it?" "Are you aware of God now?" There is no right answer. Several stock questions are: "Did you ask God?" "What was God's response?" "Where is the call of God in that?"*

    - Contemplative remarks: *"You noticed God's presence or absence in the story." "When you talked about that, your face really lit up. It seemed to me there was great joy in you." "It's really frustrating when God seems to be absent."*

3. *The* observer. *You aren't part of the conversation at all. The speaker and listener shouldn't look at you.*

    - Keep time: *Announce when time is running out ("you've got a minute to go").*

- Observe the speaker: *What is being said beyond the words? What questions might you ask? Where do you notice God? Observe the listener. How well does he or she track and reflect? How spirit-led is the listening?*
- Observe the process: *Where is the Holy Spirit at work in each, in the dialogue, in you as you listen?*
- At the end: *ask both speaker and listener to report on their experience, and then share your observations.*[4]

When the triad is used for a spiritual conversation in this fashion, the observer plays an important role in helping the dialogue to stay grounded and to avoid projection and counter-projection. While speaker and listener can get caught up in the feelings of the moment, the observer can remain more detached from the lure of self-deception and may discern more keenly where the movements of the conversation move toward or away from God's aims for mutual well-being. The speaker's and listener's *subjective* feelings of God's leading may be compared with the observer's more *objective* reading of God's presence in the dialogue, so that both the interior and exterior signs of God are honored. When the triad is used for a full session of mutual spiritual direction, each of the three participants should get a chance to be speaker, listener, and observer.

Checking Out

When a group has gathered and created a sacred space for mutual discernment, whether it be for worship, for study, for business, or for fellowship, it is important to close that sacred space again before leaving. When a group has checked in, it is important to check out again when the group's work is done. The checkout need not be elaborate or lengthy, but it should give the group an opportunity to look back over the time spent together, to discern how God has been at work in the work they have done and consider what aims and lures God has opened up before them as a result of the group meeting.

A simple form of checkout is to go around the table, or to let members speak at will, addressing just those questions: "What have you felt God doing here with us? What will you do next in response to God's call?" Responses should be brief, not overly analytical, and attentive to new possibilities that God creates from the past moments of the meeting.

Another form of checkout seeks to sum up the group's meeting in prayer. The prayer leader can thank God for God's presence and guidance during the group's time together and invite each member to give thanks for the particular movement of the Spirit they felt in the meeting, and ask God's empowerment for the next steps they will take. The prayer time may conclude with a simple dismissal or blessing.

A kind of checkout I use at the end of our Sunday liturgies is the "so what moment." At the end of the prayers, before the closing hymn, after all the parish announcements, I ask the congregants, "So what? We have heard scripture readings, we have sung hymns, we have shared bread and wine, we have prayed—what difference does it make?" I invite worshipers to think of a particular moment in the service that *did* make a difference to them, a moment when they felt God's presence or the Spirit's empowerment; perhaps in a song, or in the face of a friend, or in passing the Peace to someone with whom they need reconciliation; and I invite them to take that moment with them in memory, to return to it in the week to come, to pray and think and respond to that moment, because it will make a difference to how they act and how they pray and who they are in the days ahead. The so what moment helps each worshiper to reflect on the shared experience of the liturgy, and to discern in the midst of others where God has been at work in them.

In a process-relational world, God's omnipresence, omni-activity, and omni-responsiveness are the ultimate environment in which we live and move and have our being. God's calls to us and aims for us are the primordial threads from which we weave our lives. Practices of discernment help us to become more aware of and more responsive to God's call, for ourselves and for the groups to which we belong, in the continuing Holy Adventure of Creation.

Notes

1. Alan Jones, "Liturgy and Spirituality," Catacomb Cassettes (Atlanta: Episcopal Radio/TV Foundation, 1983).
2. John Ackerman, *Listening to God: Spiritual Formation in Congregations* (np: The Alban Institute, 2001).
3. Ackerman 129–30.
4. Ackerman 147–48.

PART THREE

7

Whitehead and Spiritual Discipline
John B. Cobb, Jr.

8

A Spirituality of Compassion
Bruce G. Epperly

9

Communion in Compassion
Paul S. Nancarrow

SEVEN

Whitehead and Spiritual Discipline

John B. Cobb, Jr.

IN CHAPTER FOUR, I argued that John Wesley is a good guide to a healthy Christian spirituality because he accents love of fellow creatures, especially human neighbors. I proposed that we can and should go further than he in loving our bodies and nonhuman creatures. Some Christian spiritualities lead their practitioners to devalue and control their bodies and to turn attention away from the world. They do so because of some quite widespread views of God and the human spirit. The spirit is thought to be the "highest" part of the human, and God is depicted as "above." The body and the world are below. To become more spiritual is to rise from the world toward God. These images have played a large role in Christian spirituality. Luther no doubt shared some of this imagery, but he opposed the resulting spirituality. He believed that the Christian life is to be lived in the world and not by rising above it. Today, many of us reject the imagery more fundamentally. We oppose the devaluation of the body and the natural world. We believe that biblical thought prizes God's physical creation and calls on us to do likewise.

Wesley followed Jesus in the call for love of God and neighbor, and as Christians, we should be wary of a spirituality that neglects this central teaching of our faith. But we should recognize that this "love of God" is more difficult to understand and to practice than love of neighbor. Wesley's own understanding of loving God had two foci. One was a subjective feeling of love toward God, which Wesley sometimes acknowledged that he in fact lacked. The other was a set of distinctly religious practices. In these he was very faithful, but he feared that he too often went through them without the crucial emotion.

I want to make two suggestions. First, it is a mistake to separate love of God and love of neighbor as Wesley did. The New Testament holds them much closer together. We cannot love the One we have not seen if we do not love the neighbor whom we have seen. Further, God rejoices with creaturely rejoicing and suffers with creaturely suffering. God is in the world, and all creatures are in God. Wesley recognized all of these points. But he did not draw the conclusion that the way we express love of God is by serving God's creatures. If we love all God's creatures, we do love God. The spiritual practice of extending and deepening our love of creatures also extends and deepens our love of God.

Second, however, to love God is to attend to what God is doing in the world and especially in ourselves. To attend to it also means to trust it and open ourselves so as to enable God's work to be more effective in us. It means to be grateful to God realistically for what God is most particularly engaged in doing.

The question then becomes, what is God doing? Where can we realistically discern God's working? Over the centuries, the official teaching of the church has been that God does everything. That is, nothing happens except according to the divine will. This teaching of divine omnipotence has been disastrous. We are asked to love the God who causes, or at least permits, all the horrendous evils of human history, as well as the accidents that kill small children, the cancer that attacks our loved ones, and the pain and suffering that we all endure individually. The call to love this God is often connected with threats of what happens if we do not, rather than with spontaneous gratitude for all that God has done for us. The expression of such love is as likely to be resignation in the face of evil as seeking its reduction in particular cases.

Wesley, thankfully, avoided the language of omnipotence. This was chiefly because of its connection, logical and historical, with the idea that God chooses some people to be saved and most to be damned. Wesley began his theology with the idea of God's love, and he could not reconcile that love with such massive and ultimate injustice. In understanding what God is doing in the world, he focused overwhelmingly on how God works within us to increase our faith and especially our love. We can contribute to our own growth in love by opening ourselves to the working of God within us.

Nevertheless, there is more to be said, and I find great help in Whitehead's philosophy for saying it. Whitehead provides a theory for how God participates in the constitution of human experience moment by moment. As important as this is—that our own capacity for love increases as an outcome of God's working—it does not exhaust what God is doing. Also, a theory of how God participates in us enables us to focus our attention more clearly on that working, and is, in itself, a loving of God.

In my previous discussion of how Whitehead helps to open us to the reality of God, I only noted that Whitehead opened the way to a realistic affirmation that we experience God by emphasizing the nonsensory nature of experience. Given the widespread dominance of the view that sense experience is the primary mode of experience, this is a truly important point. But Whitehead goes further. He does not just remove this radical barrier to talk of experiencing God; he develops a theory of the role God plays in creaturely experience.

In Chapters One and Four, I emphasized that every moment of human experience is a coming together of all that has happened in the past. In Whitehead's language, the many become one. This is very similar to what Buddhists understand by dependent origination. No entity exists in itself apart from other things. Each exists only in its relations. We saw how that can help us understand and develop compassion.

But for Whitehead this is not a sufficient account of what happens in the becoming of an occasion of experience. If this were all, then the new experience would be simply the vector resultant of past events. This world composed of events would be just as deterministic as the Cartesian world of material things. Although many people espouse views that imply a complete determinism, no one can in fact live or think as if this were so. We know that we make choices. We experience thinking as an effort to make right choices about what to think. We blame people for making choices that do harm to others. We feel responsible ourselves. We engage in spiritual practices for the purpose of shaping ourselves in ways more conformal to what we understand to be God's purposes for us.

But how is this possible? Typically modern thought assumes that to explain what happens is to show why it had to happen. The explanation is sought in the context or conditions of the event. This is constituted of antecedent events. If we can find nothing in these circumstances that caused the feature of the new event we are seeking to explain, then the only alternative is usually thought to be "chance." What does not happen by necessity happens by chance.

But to say that I act or think as I do "by chance" does not explain any of the phenomena of which I have spoken. I am not responsible for what happens by chance. To engage in spiritual disciplines is a choice, not simply the product of deterministic forces. There has to be something else besides determination by the past and chance.

This something else can only be self-determination. In addition to what is widely recognized as determination by the past there must also be another determination that occurs in the act of becoming. Whitehead asserts that every occasion decides just what it will become. It is important to recognize that this is not the determination of one occasion of my experience by the decision of the preceding occasion. That would still leave us with a deterministic system. It must be that in the immediacy of the becoming of a single, momentary occasion of human experience, there is a decision about how to constitute oneself.

But that, too, requires explanation. A decision can be made only if there are alternate possibilities. The past, however, does not provide possibilities. It lays on the present the obligation to conform. That is how it is causally efficacious. The present does not decide what its past is or how that past will exercise efficient causation upon it. That is given.

Whitehead's theory is that in addition to these physical or conformal feelings of the past, an occasion also has mental or conceptual feelings of relevant possibilities. It can, therefore, either simply conform to the past or decide to respond to that past in a way that introduces some difference, some novelty. In fact, Whitehead notes that sheer repetition is rare. The simple elements of the world, such as light, have a vibratory character. Each event largely repeats the past but also introduces a contrast to the immediate past. In this simplest case, the next occasion reverts to the earlier pattern. Whitehead thinks that this vibration, in distinction from sheer repetitiveness, gives some intensity to each photonic occasion.

In human experience, on the other hand, the newness in one occasion of experience opens the way to additional novelty in successive occasions. We do not normally revert to earlier patterns. What was novel at one point is now inherited from earlier occasions as increasingly entrenched in our character or capacities. We can build on it in new occasions. Even the attitude of compassion toward the enemy, so hard to achieve at first, can become part of our character.

The next question is how possibilities relevant to the past, but not derived from the past, can enter into the new occasion. Whitehead believed that there cannot be a realm of such possibilities organizing themselves and presenting themselves to us apart from something actual. He believed that only actual entities can act. Hence he posited a cosmic actual entity that includes the whole realm of possibility in such a way that it is ordered to the needs of the world. The ordering of possibilities is the basis for the order of the world as well as for the emergence of novelty and self-determination in the world. He called this actual entity "God."

More specifically, he called this the "Primordial Nature" of God. His theory was that in addition to the sphere of possibility ordered by God's conceptual feelings, God, like creaturely occasions, has physical feelings. That is, God prehends the world as well as the possibilities for the world. That is why what we do to creatures we do also to God. God's feeling of the world is integrated with God's feeling of possibilities for the world. Whitehead calls this integration the "Consequent Nature" of God. Whitehead suggests that the ordering of possibilities for our realization is affected by God's internalization of our past experience. He calls this the particular providence for particular occasions. God so orders the sphere of possibilities that every occasion feels some limited set of these possibilities and feels lured toward realizing the best. Whitehead calls this the "initial aim" derived from God. In more familiar biblical language, we can say that God calls each of us to respond creatively to our particular past in a way that will realize the greatest possible value. But God does not force us to adopt the best possibility. It is offered only as one among others.

Whitehead thinks that this call always has a dual goal. First, we are called to realize value in each moment. Second, we are called to determine the present in such a way that it will contribute value to the future. Whitehead thinks of the former aspect of the goal as primarily aesthetic, the latter, as moral. But the moral aim for future occasions is primarily at their realization of aesthetic value in the future.

At least in human experience we can see that these two aspects of the aim are distinct and can be in tension. It is possible so to seek an immediate thrill that one almost ignores the consequences for the future. But normally the quest is also for an intense experience in the imminent future as well as the moment itself. What is ignored is the more remote future. It is also possible to be so oriented to security or accomplishment in the future, or even to the well-being of others, that one is willing to live rather miserably at present.

Although these tensions are real, the normal situation is one in which present enjoyment contributes to the future and is enhanced by its sense of contributing to that future. On the whole one's own good spirits contribute to one's long-term good spirits and to the good spirits of those around one. Whitehead's focus is not on the tension.

Overall and in general God calls us to widen the sphere of the future whose enhanced values we seek. That can readily be translated into the extension of our *agape* for others. We come to care for them in such a way that we try to order our lives for their benefit. As we have seen, this sometimes may require sacrifice of present enjoyment. But in Whitehead's view, God calls us to enjoy ourselves in the present as well. Sacrifice is the exceptional demand, not the normal or normative one. The ideal is the joint realization of our own happiness and the contribution to others. Self-sacrifice can never be more than the lesser of two evils, important though it may sometimes be to choose it.

The aim of God in each occasion is also at maximum compassion. Indeed, the fullness of enjoyment depends on the breadth of compassion. It is true that Whitehead here uses the language of conformation rather than compassion. Conformation is the re-feeling of the feelings of antecedent occasions. It is never perfect, because conformation to one occasion precludes full conformation to another. But there are ways to enlarge the conformation, nevertheless.

Whitehead distinguishes between the ways in which two different feelings can largely cancel each other out, on the one hand, and the ways in which they can enhance each other as contrasts, on the other. Human experience can convert oppositions into contrasts. As we grow we can entertain different ideas in such a way that they call for a larger context in which they can be seen as different but not in contradiction. This enables us to appreciate sympathetically a variety of points of view instead of simply rejecting all that differ from our own. We can feel the diverse emotions of several people together in ways that enable us to sympathize with more than one. We can also learn to understand sympathetically the acts of someone with whom we deeply disagree without abandoning our opposition.

There are additional implications of Whitehead's thought to considerd. First, let us focus on self-determination or freedom. According to Whitehead, in the most literal and radical sense, God is the giver of freedom. Freedom in the Christian tradition is often understood on two levels. First, there is metaphysical freedom, that is, simply the possibility of choosing. Second, the freedom in which Christians are most interested is the freedom to choose rightly. Luther and Calvin denied that we naturally possess any such freedom. We are by nature sinners. We do not love as we should, and we are unable, on our own, to attain to any such love.

Wesley agreed that on our own, in terms of exclusively human nature, we are not free to do what is right. But Wesley believed that in real, complete human beings, we are never alone. God's grace participates in constituting our personhood. Because of the working of God's grace in us, we can become loving persons.

Whitehead supports Wesley here. If we view an actual occasion of a human life apart from God's work in it, it can do nothing good. At most it can only be what it is made to be by the past. But in fact there is no actual occasion that is constituted only by the effects of the past. Every occasion is constituted by the joint working of past occasions and of God. Each culminates in a decision. That decision is likely to fall short of God's ideal aim for the occasion, for it is influenced by many factors. But one cannot specify any necessity that it always fall short or that it fall short by any particular degree. The occasion will conform to some extent to God's aim for it. It may conform to a considerable extent. That will mean that God's grace has been wonderfully effective in affecting the decision. We need to be sensitively aware of our falling short and missing the mark. But we can also celebrate the achievements of God in our hearts and seek to become increasingly responsive.

To work with God is to exercise the metaphysical freedom God gives us moment by moment as fully as we can and as much in accordance with God's call as possible. All our discussion of compassion and agape give more concrete content to what this means. But there is also a sense of adventure that can be missed if we do not attend to it. God calls us to open ourselves to ways of being and doing that go beyond what we have thought of and enjoyed in the past. God calls us to think thoughts that may be in tension with our past beliefs.

In the tradition, some forms of spirituality were concerned to silence voices that were not in accord with what was understood as orthodoxy. For example, the idea that God is not omnipotent—an idea I emphasized earlier—would be regarded as a demonic proposal to be resisted and fought against. If God calls us into novelty, on the other hand, this clinging to received beliefs is opposing God's call.

Obviously, that does not mean that every new idea is better than old ones. Some may even be silly and evil. But most serious new ideas have reasons for being proposed. They explain some things better than the ideas they want to replace. God calls us to openness toward them. The aim is not simply to judge them better or worse than other ideas. The aim is to enlarge the range of ideas that we understand and appreciate so that we can develop a larger vision that makes sense of more of them.

There is biblical warrant for understanding this expansion of thought positively. In the New Testament we are repeatedly told that the fullness of understanding belongs to the future. In context, this idea is apocalyptic, but it has a more general relevance. Our present knowledge is vague and limited. There is much truth that God can reveal to us over time as we become ready to learn it. Whitehead does not support the idea of a final consummation when all truth is wholly revealed, but he certainly supports the idea that our present knowledge is fragmentary and that God calls us to learn more and more.

For Jews, study of the Torah is the major form of spirituality. For Christians, study of the Bible, to a much lesser extent, plays an important role. But for Christians, even more than for Jews, this study itself points toward learning from others. Interfaith dialogue is an important spiritual practice in our time.

Let us consider, then, what kind of spiritual discipline is appropriate with respect to God's gift of novelty. I think we can attend from time to time to the more dramatic novelties that have presented themselves to us. Some of them we have, no doubt, appropriated. For these we can give thanks. You may think that they are the gifts of other people rather than of God. But our ability to appropriate them is part of God's continuing working within us. We may ask ourselves also how well we have integrated these novel ideas with our other convictions. If that integration is not well developed, then we can experience the call to engage in that activity.

The more important question is about ideas that have felt threatening. They would not be threatening if they lacked plausibility. We need to ask what we fear and why we fear it. We need to try to open ourselves more fully to understanding and examining the ideas. They may prove vague and unimportant or fallacious. In that case, we can largely dismiss them. But if they prove to be serious claimants on our credulity, then we must deal more directly with the ways they threaten our existing belief system. Is there a larger vision that can include the truth of the new idea along with the truth of our previous beliefs? Whitehead's philosophy and, I think, the Bible, give us reason to think that there is. Truth is one, and the fullness of truth contains all the truths that are to be found in separated form. Incorporating new truths brings us closer to that remote completeness of truth that is realized only in God. Moving through this process expresses love of God.

There is another type of spirituality that warrants consideration. In a broad sense, Whitehead supports notions of providence and even of personal guidance. Wesley occasionally sought divine guidance in ways that his own theology did not justify. That is, he would open the Bible at random and with closed eyes put his finger on a verse. He would then suppose that he could learn God's specific will from this verse. This method belongs with the enthusiast's view of the relation of God and the world. It assumes that when the human being is relatively passive, God is more determinative of what happens.

That is not Wesley's basic view. He did not invite his followers to wait passively for God to give them faith and love. Quite the contrary, he encouraged active participation in achieving the needed transformation of life. He opposed what he called quietism. Hence Wesley's occasional practice in this regard does not belong to a Wesleyan spirituality.

Whitehead's model certainly does not support that kind of practice. But his passing reference to a particular providence for particular occasions does suggest that God provides guidance moment by moment. Does this mean that when we feel particularly unsure of what we should do, we can get an answer from God?

The answer from Whitehead is not clear. It seems that there

is a theoretical possibility of such conscious guidance, but there is no clear indication whether this would ever be realized. The possibility is left at the empirical or historical level. Do people in fact experience such guidance? Some certainly feel that they do. On this point, as on many others dealing with extraordinary experience, Whitehead leaves open the possibility.

However, in general, guidance functions in a much less explicit or conscious way. It does not involve the transmission of information. Whitehead believes that we are vaguely aware of a rightness partly realized and partly missed. Sometimes the missing is felt in quite acute and painful ways. On the other hand, sometimes we have a sense of moving with the spirit with little tension. In the midst of creative work, sometimes an artist feels identified with a kind of inspiration that works through her.

Some people seem to be more comfortably aligned with the creative possibilities, whereas others resist being drawn out of deep habitual ruts. Spiritual disciplines can help us to move in the former direction. Largely these are the disciplines already described.

But a distinct discipline of listening to the call of God may also be appropriate. Here, great caution must be observed. In every moment there are many impulses coming to us from the past: from our bodies, from our memories, from other people. Some are good and some are bad. Many may be stronger and more conscious than the call of God.

It is all too easy to mistake one or another for God's call.

It is, on the whole, safer to identify the direction in which God always calls us and to concentrate on moving in that direction. As we do so we reduce the obstacles within ourselves to the effective working of God's Spirit. This means that we can seek to become more compassionate and extend the scope of those whose well-being we truly desire and seek to support. We can open ourselves to the new and work to integrate the new with the old, thereby transforming both.

But there are times when we are faced with momentous decisions and our compassion and agape and openness to the new do not tell us which way to go. One response is "to let go and let God." This should not be interpreted as supporting Wesley's method of leaving it to God to place his finger on the appropriate biblical verse. But when rational reflection does not answer our question, we may be able to trust a certain spontaneity, moment by moment, through which the larger decision will, in fact, be made. Looking back we can often see in our own lives how things worked out beyond any planning or clear decision on our part. The more open and loving we are, the more effectively God's call can work in us apart from conscious awareness on our part. Day by day Christian living is primarily of this sort. The big decisions may be made in this way as well.

None of this excludes the possibility that God's call may sometimes become a conscious element in our experience. The Jesuits have developed the discipline of discerning the spirits. They recognize that experience is informed by many sources and that we are easily deceived as to which impulse or message is from God. But they believe that there are procedures for discernment, involving a group of believers and not simply a single person, that achieve relatively reliable results. Their work is mature, sensitive, and wise. It can be interpreted and appreciated from a Whiteheadian point of view.

Among Protestants it is the Quakers who have developed the quest for divine guidance most sensitively. They, too, know the danger of treating some hunch or unconscious desire as if it were a divine call. They, too, recognize that such efforts to gain specific guidance presuppose Christian maturity. They, too, understand the importance of individuals submitting their judgments to group consideration. Whiteheadian Wesleyans, if they wish to learn the art of discerning the spirits, can turn to Jesuits and Quakers.

Of course there are times of crisis in which these elaborate disciplines are not practicable. And there is a kind of hothouse Wesleyan piety, a certain intensity of faith in divine providence, which gives rise to many stories of remarkable guidance. I am fascinated by these stories. I suspect that the positive instances are much more reported than the negative ones, but I do not disparage the positive stories on that account.

I will conclude by telling you of a woman from a small Georgia town whom I grew up calling Cousin Mary Culler. She was a cousin of my grandfather. In the late nineteenth century she went as a Methodist missionary to the interior of China alone. She was, without doubt, a woman of great faith and extreme intimacy with God. This made her a most formidable person to contend with. But she used her striking spiritual power in love.

I enjoy telling a story about her during the Japanese invasion of China. It happened that Bishop Arthur J. Moore, who oversaw the missionary work of the Southern Methodist Church throughout East Asia, was in Shanghai. Someone came to him in great agitation, saying, "Mary Culler White and scores of her Bible-women are on Mount Mokanshan, and the Japanese are taking the mountain. What shall we do?" I do not need to remind you, I suspect, of the reputation the Japanese army acquired for its treatment of civilian women in China. Bishop Moore knew Mary Culler White well. His answer was: "I'm sorry, there is nothing we can do. The Japanese will just have to look out for themselves." And he was right. Cousin Mary Culler handled the situation with no help from anyone but God.

I have several books she wrote about her experiences. They are full of accounts of remarkable divine guidance and providence. Knowing her, and knowing that some of her achievements are difficult to understand in any other way, I do not discount her understanding of the events. I have no doubt that she tells the stories honestly, whatever factors may have been at work of which she was ignorant. I am sure God was at work.

I close with this because I think it is important for those of us who think of ourselves as sophisticated and enlightened not to dismiss the miracle stories of the Bible and the miracles that occur in our own time. If God is at work in all things, we should not set limits on what that working can do and be. But for the vast majority of us, it is unwise to seek such dramatic miracles in daily life. The miracle of trust and openness and love is enough. If we seek first the *basileia theou,* the Commonwealth of God and God's righteousness, we do not know what more will be given to us.

EIGHT

A Spirituality of Compassion

Bruce G. Epperly

PROCESS SPIRITUALITY is grounded in a metaphysical vision that affirms the dynamic interrelatedness of life, the omnipresence of God, and the ubiquitous reality of divine inspiration. Every moment of experience creatively embraces and transforms the world from which it arises. Every encounter reveals not only the intentions and actions of oneself and others but also the purposes of God within that situation. Within every moment of experience and relationship, God seeks to inspire wholeness, liveliness of experience, and reconciliation in the microcosm as well as the macrocosm. Every moment and every encounter is an "icon," a window through which we may experience God's lively presence. Despite the realities of violence, alienation, and conflict, all moments reveal at their deepest level God's ever-present "sighs too deep for words."

Process theology affirms the wisdom of Mother Teresa, who recognized God's presence hidden within persons left to die on the streets of Calcutta. Like Michelangelo, whose artistic vision identified holiness in unexpected places, process theology sees angels in life's boulders— in the painful jagged moments of life as well as in those persons whom we define as "enemies." We can experience divine inspiration as we gaze at the heavens and as we peer deeply into the gnarled face on Christ in one of his many disguises. We can experience divine revelation through imaginative meditation on the faces of Saddam Hussein and George Bush as well as the touch of the beloved, the kind words from a friend, or an insightful passage from scripture or a devotional text.

Thomas Merton once invited persons to practice "contemplation in a world of action." This is the spiritual challenge at the heart of ethics and social transformation. Profoundly committed to healing the world, process theology also recognizes that social transformation and spiritual leadership require us to act from a quiet center. In my own work with activist pastors, I have observed the potential for stress-related illness, burnout, and political polarization among these open-hearted advocates for social justice and planetary healing. Lacking an awareness of God's presence in our own lives, we often fail to see the holy in others—to use the language of Buber, our opponent becomes an "it" rather than a "thou." Sadly, in listening to the cries of the poor, social activists and religious leaders often neglect the equally important voices of their own spouses, children, or partners. Overwhelmed by the task of healing the world, we succumb to hopelessness and anxiety. We forget the divine wellspring of energy and inspiration that is our deepest reality.

In the midst of conflict, process theology reminds us that, despite the perceived recalcitrance of our opponent, God is working within her or his life. Our prayers for national leaders and political opponents enable God's holy desire for shalom to have a greater impact on their lives. Accordingly, for those who attend to God's aim at wholeness in their relationships, political action becomes an opportunity for reconciliation and spiritual transformation as well as social change. As Walter Wink notes, the future belongs to the intercessors. Our prayers, like the "butterfly effect," radiate across the universe, subtly changing those situations for which we pray and in which we act.

A well-known aphorism calls us to "think globally and act locally." Concern for the wider realities of global warming, sustainable economics, justice among nations, and nuclear proliferation needs to be balanced by healthy relationships in the family, workplace, and congregation. Sadly, many activists neglect their own well-being and the well-being of their most significant relationships with spouses, partners, friends, and children. Healing the planet must simultaneously occur with the healing of our personal, relational, and communal lives. Aware of the profound connection of person and planet, Jewish mystics proclaimed that the healing of one soul—beginning with our own—transforms and heals the universe. Process spirituality affirms that an ever-flowing wellspring of divine energy and centeredness is available at all times and places for those who open themselves to God.

Whitehead describes peace as a widening of the self and its concerns to include wider and wider circles of relationships. Similarly, in the language of Paul's letter to the Corinthians, authentic peace emerges when we truly experience ourselves within the dynamic relatedness of the body of Christ, in which our well-being is intimately related to every other member. Further, in the context of process spirituality and theology, God can be described as the lively mind or spirit that permeates and reveals itself in every cell of the cosmic body. In the intricate relatedness of the psychosomatic universe, we can truly affirm that as we have done unto the least of these, we have done unto God. In the body of Christ, authentic spirituality affirms that my healing is connected with the healing of the whole.

Our greatest challenge in the embodiment of a spirituality of compassion in the rough and tumble world of social change is to, on the one hand, trust God's adventurous presence in the world beyond our own efforts and, on the other hand, to experience God in the midst of our efforts at social transformation. This challenge is captured in an inscription found on a bench at the Kirkridge Retreat and Conference Center—"picket and pray!" From the privacy of our times of prayer, we are called to pray even as we canvass for political causes, volunteer for a soup kitchen or Habitat for Humanity, or advocate for universal healthcare in the United States.

Healing begins at home. We must deal with our own inner violence and conflict if we are to be instruments of peace amid the communal and global conflicts of our time. Process spirituality affirms the wisdom of Gandhi and King, who asserted the importance of "soul force" or "spiritual centeredness" in political and social change.

Peace of spirit arises from our participation in communities of wholeness that provide practices of inner peace along with personal support and accountability for their members. These practices of inner peace allow God's aim at wholeness to flow through us toward others.

Centering prayer. Medical studies have found that contemplative prayer calms both the spirit and the body. When we take 15 minutes for quiet prayer, we experience a reduction of stress that is reflected in lower blood pressure, greater immune system function, and the experience of higher creativity. Our inner calm radiates across the universe bringing peace to conflict situations.

The practice of centering prayer is present in virtually every religious tradition. It combines spiritual focus with gracefulness toward oneself. It reminds us that we can remain centered amid the storms of political and interpersonal conflict.

> *Take a few moments simply to be still in a relaxed position, breathing in God's peace from head to toe. In the quiet moment, open yourself to divine guidance and care.*

> *Centered in God, take a moment to focus on your prayer word. This can be any word that is spiritually significant to you ("God," "love," "peace," "joy," "Christ," "Jesus," "Sophia," "Shalom," "light," etc.) If you experience interruptions or random thoughts, simply return to your focus without self-criticism or judgment.*

> *Close with a prayer for inner and outer peace. Take 15–20 minutes, ideally twice a day.*

Breath prayer. In Chapter Two, I introduced the role of breath prayer in spiritual and physical centering. As Thich Nhat Hanh reminds us "peace is every step."[1] In the spirit of the Vietnamese Buddhist monk, I would add that "peace is every breath." In the dynamic flow of life, our breath aligns us with God's Breath of Life, moving through all things. In the Divine Breath, all things are embraced, loved, and eventually transformed. Holy Breath connects us with our spiritual guides. We breathe the same energetic breath that enlightened Gautama the Buddha and that radiated through the hands of Jesus the healer.

The tasks of compassionate social action can overwhelm us. Our efforts seem meager, our time finite. Like Martha of the gospel story, we can become anxious and forget our highest purpose. Our anxiety and defensiveness can lead to polarization and emotional violence. Accordingly, conscious breathing enables us to stay in touch with God's aim at wholeness and peace in every situation of conflict. It also reminds us that we are not called to be successful, but to be faithful to God's holy desire. Though we may not complete our task, our efforts contribute to planetary healing and are eternally treasured by God.

Holy breathing. Simply respond to each encounter with full and deep breathing.

> *Your breath connects you with the Wisdom (Sophia) of God, the healing of Jesus, the insight of Gautama, the devotion of Mary of Magdala, the passionate social action of Dorothy Day, the peaceful nonresistance of King and Gandhi, the flexible green spirit of Hildagard of Bingen.*
>
> *As the phone rings, breathe...*
>
> *As you experience yourself overwhelmed by the tasks of social justice and transformation at home, breathe...*
>
> *As you experience anxiety in unfamiliar situations, breathe...*
>
> *As anger rises, breathe...*
>
> *As the desire to say a word that will cut another down to size, breathe...*
>
> *Let the peace of God breathe within you with every breath.*

Process spirituality embraces the spirit of what Walter Bruggemann has described as the prophetic imagination, the ability to envisage a creative alternative to the present condition of injustice. Prophetic healing embraces our own personal healing as we seek to heal our communities and the planet. Our healing visions arise from and are fulfilled through their embodiment in life's most challenging situations. In such situations, we seek to intuit God's aim—the highest aim in that moment, "the best for the impasse." Although the best for the impasse may not be ideal and may involve conflict, its embodiment leads to the next step in personal and communal healing and paves the way for deeper social and planetary transformation.

Finding Angels in Boulders. The story is told of the sculptor Michelangelo. One day, a neighbor observed him rolling a jagged boulder up the hill to his front porch. When Michelangelo began to hammer on the boulder, the neighbor was overcome with curiosity. "Why are you pounding on that boulder?" he asked. To which the sculptor replied, "there's an angel inside, and I'm trying to set it free." Indeed, if you look at Michelangelo's drawings, you can see angelic figures leaping out of misshapen stones.

Finding angels in boulders is essential to prophetic healing and compassionate spirituality. The following spiritual exercise enables us to see God's presence in its often-disguised forms. It can be practiced in a marriage, a friendship, parenting, or the political arena.

> *Take a few minutes simply to be still. Open yourself to God's holy desire for this particular time in your life.*
>
> *When you feel rested and at peace, you may begin to practice this exercise.*
>
> *Imagine a heavy, jagged, misshapen boulder. What does it look like? What challenges do you see in creating something of beauty out of this jagged material? In the artistry of your life, what thing of beauty might you bring forth from this jagged boulder?*
>
> *How would you go about coaxing beauty from this boulder? Imagine the finished product. What does it look like?*
>
> *Take a moment to imagine some person who you are tempted to see as a boulder in your life. What does he or she look like? In what*

ways do his or her jaggedness cause you or others pain or discomfort? Take some time to look deeper into the other: are you able to see any goodness in her or him? Can you see a glimmer of the divine in the boulder? As an artist of life, in what ways can you assist in bringing forth the angelic from this person?

Now take a few minutes to recognize the boulders in your own life—your own jagged edges. Let the divine artist work in your life to bring forth your own angelic reality. What does it look like?

Conclude by thanking the divine artist for enabling the angelic to come forth in you and the life of others.

Commit yourself to seeing and acting in partnership with God's aim at wholeness.

Seeing Christ in the "least of these." Jim Wallis of Sojourners tells the story of a particularly good-spirited woman who works at a soup kitchen in Washington, D.C. She greets each person who goes down the food line with a smile and a kind word, regardless of their demeanor, appearance, or smell. When she was asked why she was so affirmative to persons going down the line, she responded, "One day, Jesus is coming down this line, and I want to treat him real good."

Process spirituality affirms that Christ is present to us in every encounter. On the one hand, God's presence is the deepest, albeit hidden, reality of everyone we meet. On the other hand, every encounter is embraced in the divine receptivity. Truly each encounter gives us the opportunity, as Mother Teresa proclaims, to do "something beautiful for God" by contributing something of beauty to God's experience of the world.

The following spiritual exercise, based on Matthew 25:31–46, can be practiced as an imaginative prayer. But, this exercise becomes life-transforming when we pause a moment to experience God's presence in every- one we meet.

> *Take a few moments to read or listen to Matthew 25:31–46 with particular focus on experiencing God in the "least of these."*
>
> *In your imagination, envisage the people mentioned in this passage. Envisage someone who is hungry. What do they look like? How has hunger shaped their lives? Now, look beyond their hunger to see the holy in their lives. How can you best respond to their need? See yourself responding to their need as if you are giving to God.*
>
> *Envisage someone who is thirsty. What do they look like? How has thirst shape their lives? Now, look beyond their thirst to see the holy in their lives. How can you best respond to their need? See yourself responding to their need as if you are giving to God?*
>
> *In like manner, repeat this exercise…envisaging one who is without adequate clothing…who is ill…and who is in prison. Open to God's presence in their lives and experience God's joy at receiving your generosity.*
>
> *Now, take a moment to experience your own lack…those places where you are in need of comfort and warmth, of support and counsel. Imagine one who has served you, responding to your deepest needs. Accept her or his gift gratefully and lovingly.*
>
> *As you conclude, review the faces of those whom you supported, giving thanks for the opportunity to share. Envisage the one who supported you, giving thanks for their generosity and the mutuality of giving and receiving.*

Practicing this exercise delivers us from another type of

polarization, that which divides giver and receiver. In the intricate web of life, giving and receiving are profoundly interconnected. We dehumanize those to whom we give if we experience them only in terms of their deficiency or lack. They become objects of our generosity, rather than subjects of God's love. Within the intricate fabric of relationships, I cannot experience wholeness unless you find wholeness, and you cannot find wholeness without my realization of wholeness. Within the body of Christ—the intricate divine community which embraces not only the church but all reality—we are ultimately united in such a way that "if one member suffers, all suffer together with it; if one member is honored, all rejoice together with it" (I Corinthians 12:26).

Process spirituality presents a vision of reality characterized by dynamic-creative-evolving interdependence in which all things reflect God's Holy Adventure. Within God's evolving adventure, we are called to be messengers and partners in healing the world. We cannot heal the world unless we see our lives immerse in a personal and planetary healing process.

Dorotheos of Gaza once described the spiritual journey as a circle in which each person's life is represented by a point on the circumference of the circle. The course of our spiritual journey can be described as a line leading from the circumference to the divine center. In this holy circle, the closer we are to God, the closer we are to our neighbor. Conversely, the closer we are to our neighbor, the closer we are to God. Process spirituality proclaims a "metaphysics of love" in which our spiritual growth is measured by our commitment to bringing beauty and love to the world. The following exercises are intended to awaken us to the interconnectedness of life and inspire our commitment to bringing wholeness to the world, both human and nonhuman.

Vines and branches. Jesus once spoke of the life of faith in terms of our conscious participation in a Divine Vine that embraces all creation (John 15:1, 4–5). God's energy flows through us giving life and growth to all things. As we share in Divine energy, we bring beauty and life to the whole earth.

In this exercise in imaginative prayer, we affirm the interconnectedness of God in all things and our role in healing creation.

Begin with a time of quiet contemplation, followed by the reading of John 15:1, 4–5.

Imagine a lovely, green, and lively vine through which a holy energy is constantly flowing. What does the vine look like?

Experience yourself as a branch on this lively vine. Experience the lively energy of the vine flowing through the branch. What is it like to experience the divine energy? What blocks the energy of the vine? What are the consequences of blocking the energy?

Experience the energy of the vine flowing through you, eliminating any blocks.

Filled with divine energy, what type of fruit are you bearing? Now, look beyond your particular branch. What other branches are there on the vine?

Can you identify them with any persons in your life? What sort of fruit are they bearing?

In what ways do these other branches contribute to your life? In what way do you contribute to their well-being?

Experience God's energy flowing through every branch, joining all things and bringing forth fruit of all kinds.

Praying the World. In this imaginative prayer, we focus on the healing of all things with the recognition that our prayers create a healing "field of force" that is completed in our contemplative actions.

> *Take time to be still, immersing ourselves in profound interconnectedness of life, with each breath. Begin with our own spiritual center, breathing in God's presence in terms a healing light. Experience God's healing light filling your mind, body, spirit, and emotions. Experience your wholeness in the divine light.*
>
> *Imagine that light expanding to embrace a loved one . . . a good friend . . . a co-worker . . . a neighbor.*
>
> *Imagine the light further expanding to embrace your congregation . . . community . . . state . . . nation . . .*
>
> *Imagine this light extending to embrace a nation identified as your nation's enemy . . . experience this light embracing the whole Earth, bringing healing to the planet as a whole . . .*
>
> *Imagine this planet enveloping light returning toward your personal center . . . through an enemy nation . . . your nation . . . state . . . community . . . congregation . . . a neighbor . . . a co-worker . . . good friend . . . a loved one(s) . . . and yourself . . .*
>
> *Conclude by seeing all things in God's light and committing yourself to be God's partner in healing the world.*

Notes

1. Thich Nhat Hanh, *Peace Is Every Step: the Path of Mindfulness in Everyday Life* (NY: Bantam Books, 1991).

NINE

Communion in Compassion

Paul S. Nancarrow

W E HAVE SEEN that Christian spirituality is especially characterized by its goal of growth in love, *agape*, and compassion for other individuals and for the whole world. Distinctively Christian are those spiritual practices which, emulating the portrayal of Jesus in the gospels, emphasize love of God and love of neighbor—and love of God *in* neighbor. We have also seen that an emphasis on *agape* and compassion fits well with a Whiteheadian account of spirituality, which stresses relationality, interdependence, and richness of experience in mutual well-being. A Whiteheadian Christian spirituality will be particularly interested in practices which help the practitioner to grow in compassion and love.

Among spiritual practices for groups, the most important for growth in love is participation in the liturgy of Holy Communion. Norman Pittenger calls Holy Communion "the characteristically Christian thing"; he goes on to say that eucharistic worship is

> what Christianity *really is*: the adoration and service of

God decisively disclosed and released in the event of Christ, with response in faith and the enabling of the participants to share a life in love and a profound concern for the righteousness and justice which are both dependent upon and the consequence of love.[1]

The Eucharist, the Mass, the Divine Liturgy, the Lord's Supper— by whatever name it is called or in whatever particular liturgical form it is celebrated, the Holy Communion is the chief Christian symbolic expression of compassionate life in community.

The Holy Communion is "the characteristically Christian thing" for growth in *agape* and compassion because the eucharistic liturgy can draw worshipers into sharing the relationship with God that was exemplified in Jesus' own life and ministry. The eucharistic liturgy represents the forms of definiteness that were characteristic of Jesus' life and makes them available to be experienced and embodied in the contemporary lives of worshipers. In process-relational thought, a thing *is* what it *does*. A thing's existence, or a person's life, is a series of moments of experience; these moments are connected to each other by certain eternal objects—abstract qualities and past facts—that are reenacted from one moment to the next. A thing's "nature" is that constellation of eternal objects that it reenacts consistently in its moments: my desk chair is a chair because in each moment its constituent parts reenact together the quality of *chairness*; I am a human being because in each moment my body, mind, psyche, biochemistry, and so on, reenact the quality of *humanness*. Traditionally, Jesus is said to have had two "natures," human and divine; in a process-relational formulation, this can be said to mean that Jesus in his life and ministry, his person and his work, enacted both human and divine forms of definiteness. Jesus did what humans do, and that makes him human; but Jesus also did what *God* does, and that makes him divine. In his earthly ministry, Jesus not only proclaimed God's *basileia*, but Jesus enacted it, healing people as a sign of God's reign come near, liberating people from the bondage of sin and separation, breaking down barriers between people and gathering them into new communities characterized by the *agape* and compassion of divine love. Because Jesus did what only God can do, Jesus *is* God; in Jesus, humanity and divinity are not two different "substances" that must be reconciled by some metaphysical paradox, but they are two qualities of action that are effectively united in one person's acting.

The liturgical action of Holy Communion represents those qualities of Jesus' acting, through symbol and ceremony, and makes them available to become constituent elements in the lives of worshipers today. In the liturgical reading of scripture, for instance, stories that illustrate the divine-and-human qualities of Jesus are read out, to be made available for reenactment in the hearing and imagination—and action—of the hearers. Stories from the Hebrew Scriptures that shaped Jesus' own human consciousness are made available to shape the consciousnesses of Jesus' followers. In liturgical prayer, the needs and concerns and celebrations and intercessions and petitions and thanksgivings of the worshipers are brought into conscious connection with the ministerial qualities of Jesus' life and work. Especially in the Lord's Prayer, when worshipers reenact the specific words of Jesus in their own hearts and voices, the qualities of Jesus' prayer and the worshipers' prayer are brought together, so that contemporary worshipers do again as Jesus does.

It is preeminently in sharing the symbolic meal of bread and wine that the eternal objects of Jesus' life and work are made available for feeling by the gathered community. Jesus used this meal to typify his own self-giving and sharing love, and in the liturgical reenactment of the meal, the character of Jesus' love is made available to characterize the worshipers' loves as well. In Pittenger's words, in the ceremonial action,

> as in all events or occasions, the past is brought into the immediacy of present experience, asking for decision and making a difference. The originating event of Christ becomes "alive today," when the Christian community reenacts what its Lord is believed to have done at the Last Supper.[2]

When the Christian assembly in eucharistic ceremony does as Jesus does, then the real presence of Jesus is made causally efficacious in the constitution of the society and its members. The saving event of Christ is reenacted in the church community, through the symbolic signification of the ceremonial act.

The meal of bread and wine can represent the eternal objects of Jesus' life and ministry in large part because the symbolism is so rich, because there are so many layers and multiple meanings and "cross-referenced" significations in the central symbols. And in this connection it is especially important to note that the symbols are not simply the bread and wine alone, but the *actions* undertaken with the bread and wine. The Eucharist is not simply a setting-aside of bread and wine to gaze upon or contemplate, but it is a series of actions done in community and with the participation of all the members. It is the central symbolic activity of taking, blessing, breaking, and sharing which imports the defining characteristic of the *agape* and compassion of God in Christ into the present situation.

The central association, of course, is the account of Jesus' Last Supper with his disciples, when he shared bread and wine with them as signs of a new covenant instituted in his body and sealed in his blood. Sharing the bread and wine in recapitulation of Jesus' action is understood as a recapitulation of sharing in that covenant.

But the bread and the wine were hardly neutral elements when Jesus first used them; they already had complex associative overtones. The bread which Jesus named his body was an associative nexus for the whole of his ministry of service and compassion. Bread was a central sign of compassion in the miracle story of the multiplication of the loaves—one of the few miracle stories to be reported in all four canonical gospels, and so clearly of signal importance in the understanding of the early Christian community. Bread was also a sign of service in *agape* in the numerous instances of Jesus sharing table fellowship with the poor and the outcast. In sharing this bread with his disciples at their final supper, Jesus was sharing with them the whole ministry of agapeic service for the well-being of others.

Likewise, the wine of Communion bears multiple symbolic meanings. The words attributed to Jesus at the Last Supper connect the cup of wine with a "new covenant"; covenants were traditionally sealed by the shedding of sacrificial blood. The symbol of a "new covenant" is also tied to the prophetic promise of "a new heart" and "a new spirit" (see, e.g, Ezekiel 36:26–28), a new possibility and potentiality to live human lives in accordance with the compassionate and loving aims of God. The cup of wine as sign of the covenant invites those who drink it to exemplify the same qualities of compassion and love in their actions. Moreover, according to John's gospel, the first of Jesus' "signs" was the wine miracle at Cana of Galilee, where the wine was given for the sheer and simple purpose of increasing the richness of experience and abundance of well-being among the wedding guests; the sharing of that wine was an exemplification of servant ministry done in compassion. The wine of Communion thus presents a richly multilayered symbolism for the self-giving ministry of compassion in Jesus.

Furthermore, the bread and the wine together were also associated with God's promised aim for the faithful people. They were significant items in the Passover meal, commemorating God's liberating act in bringing the people of Israel out of bondage in Egypt; they were also mentioned in the prophets' imagery of the Messianic Banquet at the fulfillment of the ages in the ultimate Peace of God. Both those sets of associations are taken up, reinterpreted, and cross-referenced to new associative patterns—including liberation from bondage to death, and fulfillment of Peace in everlasting life through Jesus' death and resurrection—in this supper. The bread and the wine are not only symbols for Jesus' life and ministry, but signs of the call to compassionate life and ministry for the whole community.

And the sharing of bread and wine has associations for the worshipers as well. Bread and wine are not natural products, but are the result of the combination of wheat and grapes and human effort; the offering and sharing of bread and wine are thus symbolic of the offering and sharing of the worshipers' efforts, activities, and very selves. The bread and the wine provide a presented locus onto which the worshipers can project their own hopes and intentions and needs and desires, offering them all to be taken up and harmonized into the larger pattern of eternal objects and divine aims characteristic of Jesus' life and ministry and compassion and love. And, of course, the sharing of a meal is a very basic human gesture, prior to any particular religious interpretation or symbolism. To share a meal—even so stylized a meal as a wafer of bread and a sip of wine—is to enact a gesture of mutual regard and service, it is to embody a character of *agape* and compassion.

When Christians share this meal of bread and wine, with the added symbolism of their efforts and activities and selves, with the *further* added symbolism of the life and ministry of Christ, the entire action becomes a society of occasions in which the eternal objects exemplified in Jesus are made available for exemplification in the worshipers as well. The Holy Communion becomes a social environment in which congregants can be formed in the Spirit of Christ. The spirituality of Communion is the characteristically Christian spirituality, and spiritual practices which foster Communion in feeling and in act are characteristically important Christian practices.

I have said the liturgy of Holy Communion offers the eternal objects exemplified in Jesus to be felt and enacted in the worshipers. But for that feeling to be effective in the constitution of the worshipers' occasions of experience, the worshipers must accept the feeling of those objects, must decide to feel the objects as important as factors in their own concrescence. The ceremony is, in Pittenger's words, "a way in which we are both prehended and grasped by, and ourselves can prehend and grasp, an act which has objectively been done" in God's historical act in Christ.[3] As Jesus freely accepted God's aims for him in the course of his earthly life and ministry, so the believer in the course of the sacramental ceremony must freely accept the aims of God represented in the remembrance of Christ which the ceremony makes available. As the remembrance of Jesus' characteristic life and ministry becomes the center around which the worshiper's present feeling and action is integrated, through sacramental reenactment the Christian is conformed to Christ. As the Eucharist recalls Jesus' self-offering to communion with God, so it enables the worshiper's self-offering to communion with Christ in God through the church. The two offerings are coordinated in the liturgy, so that the worshiper's self-offering takes on the character of Christ's self-offering. The worshiper's whole person is drawn into this communion, as different aspects of the liturgical action draw out different aspects of body and psyche: the readings from scripture and sermon harbor conformation of thought to Christ; prayers of intercession and petition harbor conformation of works of compassion and justice to Christ; hymns and songs harbor conformation of emotions to Christ; even posture and gesture and sight and taste harbor conformation of the body to Christ—and this is by no means an exhaustive or exclusive list. Imagination, intellect, will, memory, emotion, sensation, and physicality are all engaged. The whole of the ceremony is the sacramental process in which the whole of the person is taken up into communion with God and instilled with godly aims and empowered for godly action. And this is repeated for every participant in the liturgy, so that the ceremonial action has an interpersonal as well as a personal significance. Because each makes a self-offering in conformance to Christ, each is conformed to the others as well, so that growing in communion with God in the remembrance of Jesus is simultaneously growing in communion with other people in the remembrance of Jesus. The qualities of *agape* and compassion that are characteristic of Jesus are exemplified in the interpersonal relationships of the whole community gathered for Communion, as well as the personal feelings and actions of each individual communicant.

The spiritual exercises that help build up a spirituality of communion, then, are those that help the worshiper *feel* the eternal objects of Jesus as re-presented in the liturgy, and then *act* on those felt objects to re-embody them in concrete occasions of compassion and love. Such exercise begins with the practices for liturgical spirituality we saw in Chapter Three: be attentive, participate fully, be mindful. The Holy Communion is, first and foremost, a liturgy, and so the general practices of liturgical spirituality are the primary means for opening oneself to the ingression of the eternal objects which the liturgy re-presents.

But the Holy Communion is also a liturgy whose specific purpose is to reenact Christ in a specific way; so there are some additional practices which may enhance and make richer the liturgical experience. These are broad suggestions for eucharistic practices; as always, they may be tailored and modified for the particulars of your individual and communal circumstances.

1. *Prepare for the liturgy.* In 1 Corinthians 11:28, Paul urges the congregation at Corinth, "Examine yourselves, and only then eat of the bread and drink of the cup." This is often taken in a strictly negative sense, indicating that we should be specifically mindful of our specific sins before receiving the sacrament given for the forgiveness of sins. The Roman Catholic custom of requiring confession before communion is an outgrowth of this interpretation of the 1 Corinthians verse. But we may also understand the verse in a broader sense. The Jesuit practice of the *examen* or examination of conscience, for instance, is intended to help us be mindful of both desolations and consolations, both those things that draw us from the love of God and those things that draw us toward the love of God. A similar sort of self-examination can be practiced before participating in Holy Communion. Prior to the service, reflect on those experiences, thoughts, feelings, actions, hopes, fears, and so on, that have come to you recently; be mindful of how those moments may have drawn you from or toward the experience and expression of Christlike love; consider how the qualities exemplified in the life and ministry of Jesus

may have changed your experience of those moments, or how those qualities might open up new possibilities to lead you from those moments to new experiences that could be even more energized by Christlike love. The liturgy of the Eucharist is intended to make the qualities of Christ available for feeling and reenactment in present life; where in *your* present life would those qualities make a difference? Making a conscious connection between life experiences and liturgical reenactment can help the worshiper to be more consciously conformed to the *agape* and compassion of Christ.

2. *Pay attention to the people involved in the service.* I noted in Chapter Two that "spiritual people-watching" can be an important part of a liturgical, corporate spirituality. This is even more important in the liturgy of Holy Communion. One of the hallmarks of Jesus' life and ministry was the way he created community around himself and among his followers. Jesus' table fellowship with everyone from tax collectors to Pharisees, fisherfolk to prostitutes, was an outward and visible sign of the inbreaking of the Commonwealth of God, a way of being together in right relationships for mutual well-being that was different from the ways of being together commonly found in the world. Some of the table fellowship stories of the Gospels emphasize further how Jesus involved others in the work of creating that fellowship: in the stories of the feeding of the thousands (Matthew 14:14–21, 15:32–38; Mark 6:34–44, 8:1–9; Luke 9:12–17), for instance, Jesus calls on his disciples to distribute the food; in John's version of the story (John 6:5–13), there is the further detail that the food originally is provided, not by the disciples, but by a young boy who offers his bread

and fish to Jesus. Jesus not only draws people together into fellowship, but Jesus also empowers others to draw people into that fellowship. This community-creating quality of Jesus' life and ministry is represented in the liturgy of Communion, in part, in the way a variety of people are called upon to act the different liturgical actions. One or two persons read the scriptures; another person leads the intercessions; other persons sing and provide musical leadership for the congregation; other persons play musical instruments; another person preaches; other persons bring the congregation's gifts of bread, wine, and money from the body of the church to the altar; other persons distribute the bread and wine at communion; one person presides, saying the Eucharistic Prayer on behalf of the whole assembly, and helping tie all the other people's actions into a coordinate liturgical work. *All* the people make responses, recite shared prayers, participate in congregational music, share the bread and the cup. The variety of ministers engaged in the liturgical ministry is a re-presentation of the quality of inclusive community exemplified in Jesus' ministry. Being intentionally mindful of the variety of ministers, noting how each brings her or his unique personal gifts and needs to the exercise of their ministry, is a way to allow that quality of Jesus to be felt and re-enacted in the present moment. The practice can help one to grow in love and compassion for others in the way of Christ.

3. *Conclude the liturgy with an intention to act.* In the story of the resurrection appearance of Jesus to two disciples on the road to Emmaus (Luke 24:13–35), the bread the disciples receive from Jesus strengthens them to get up immediately and rush back to Jerusalem to share the

good news with the whole group of disciples. One of the images often associated with the Eucharist is "food for the journey": the bread and the wine—or, more accurately, the presence of Christ communicated in the bread and the wine—are spiritual nourishment to empower us to go forth into the world and enact in the circumstances of our own lives the qualities of Christ we have received and reenacted in the symbolic space of the ceremony. In process thought, every moment of experience includes within its own satisfaction an anticipation of how it will be felt by other subsequent moments, how its accomplishment will be taken up and extended and expanded into new experiences. The experience of Holy Communion includes within itself an anticipation of how the communion-creating life and ministry of Jesus may be extended and expanded in the lives and ministries of Jesus' followers. This anticipation can be made more efficacious through conscious attention: if you think of some specific way in which you can carry the spirit of Communion out of the church and into life, some concrete circumstance in which you can do again as the Eucharist reveals Jesus to do, then that thought can serve as a spur to action, a "propositional feeling," to use Whitehead's phrase, that can lure you toward the realization of that thought in act.

In Chapter Six, I noted the "so what" moment that I use at the end of the service, It is especially relevant on Communion Sundays. At the end of each service of Holy Communion, I encourage people in the "so what" moment to form a conscious intention to act. At the end of the weekly announcements, just before the concluding hymn and dismissal out into the world, I invite everyone to think of some experience from the service—a phrase from the scriptures, an image from the sermon, the look on a person's face, a feeling elicited by one of the hymns—some experience in which they might have been aware of the Spirit of God moving them in a new way, opening up new possibilities, deepening their own sense of love and compassion in God. I then invite each person to "take that moment with you," to remember it and reflect on it and pray about it and grow into it and act in response to it through the week. Sometimes the "so what" moment leads people to commit to some particular action in the week; sometimes it leads people to intend to be more sensitive or responsive to some condition or quality. To be sure, the "so what" moments are not always profound insights, and for some may only be momentary curiosities. But the "so what" moment gives members of the congregation the opportunity to be mindful of the eternal objects of Jesus that were represented for them in the liturgical action, and to respond with an intention to re-enact those objects in their own subsequent feelings and actions in the week to come. Whether it be something so simple as a "so what" moment, or something with a more weighty commitment to a particular work or service, the effort to make a conscious intention to carry the experience of Communion forward into action in the world is an important spiritual practice for growing in the *agape* and compassion of Christ through the shared spirituality of Holy Communion.

The celebration of Holy Communion is "the characteristically Christian thing," and is a central corporate spiritual practice for growth in the *agape*, compassion, and love of God as revealed in human becoming in the life and ministry of Jesus. Mindful and intentional participation in the practices of Eucharist helps us to be conformed, as individuals and as communities, to the mission of God in Christ.

Notes

1. Norman Pittenger, *Life as Eucharist* (Grand Rapids, MI: William B. Eerdmans Publishing Co., 1973) 42; Norman Pittenger, *Freed to Love: Process Interpretation of Redemption* (Wilton, CT: Morehouse-Barlow, 1987) 100–01.
2. *Freed to Love,* 102.
3. *Freed to Love,* 104.

AFTERWORD

Marjorie Hewitt Suchocki

We have been on a journey. We have together thought deeply about what it means to live in a relational world, responding to the call of the God who is always with us. We have focused on concrete disciplines, both personal and communal. Some of these disciplines seem new; others give new insight to long accepted practice. But throughout, we have journeyed alongside John Cobb, Bruce Epperly, and Paul Nancarrow, taking them as guides on our way.

Increasing our spiritual capacity is always a journey, always a movement through our moments, creating those moments through the very dynamics of time itself. To yearn for a deeper spirituality is the creation of a journey, the shaping of our lives. The very yearning is the empowering call of the Spirit, impelling us to a deeper attentiveness to this multitudinous earth, brimming full with creatures. The Spirit calls us to integrate more of this rich otherness into ourselves, widening our very personhood through the subjectivities of others. As we respond to this call, we find ourselves awakening anew to a wider concern for the well-being of all creatures.

When I was a small child, I dutifully said my prayers each night, kneeling by my bedroom window, looking up at the stars. And I concluded my prayers with the usual "blesses," asking God please to bless my parents, my brothers, my relatives, my friends, and all creatures. But there was always a nagging worry in these petitions, for who was to bless God? So just before the "amen," I always asked God to be sure to bless God's own self.

I have since learned that God is blessed through the blessedness of all God's creatures. God experiences the world, and insofar as the world knows well-being, then God experiences the world's well-being, and God is blessed. The call of the Spirit impels us to a compassion that cares for the well-being of God's creatures, and hence to the very blessing of God. Spirituality, then, calls us each in our own way, through our own gifts, to participate in the world's good. Spirituality forces us to look to the economic processes of this world, asking how these processes affect well-being. Spirituality creates within us a political consciousness, asking how our systems of government do or do not extend the net of social care to those who are "least" among us. Spirituality generates ideas and actions that open our eyes to local policies and needs that reflect the well-being of our communities, whether through clean air and water or through affordable housing or through adequate health resources. The call of the Spirit drives us to deeper and wider care of the well-being of earth and its creatures, and in doing so, involves us in the wonder of blessing the very God who calls us.

But we do not come to such a consciousness overnight. Indeed, it is a journey of practicing the presence of God, growing accustomed to the One voice amidst the many voices—not to the cancellation of the many, but to the increasing care of the many. The journey takes our whole lives through for, by its nature, its only end point could be our full participation in the love of God and neighbor. The wonder of such an "end point" is that it intersects every moment of our lives, so that the journey is always fulfilled, yet always in process.

And so this book offers us aids for our journey—disciplines we might practice, relations we might notice, a community we might cultivate, a good we might do. But the ultimate guide to a deeper spirituality, of course, comes from God's own nudging, whether from the depths of our becoming, or from the wisdom of communities of people open to love to God and neighbor. This ultimate guide is the enabling call of the Spirit. May we respond, singly and communally, with joy and hope. In so doing, we may find ourselves exulting in the overflowing love of God that flows into our own small loves till they, too, expand and overflow. We live in gratitude for growth in our love of God and neighbor, made possible for us through the continual call of the Spirit.

www.ingramcontent.com/pod-product-compliance
Lightning Source LLC
Chambersburg PA
CBHW050320120526
44592CB00014B/1989